Thoughts on unconventional computing

Editors
Andrew Adamatzky and Louis-José Lestocart

Thoughts on Unconventional Computing

LUNIVER PRESS

Published by Luniver Press Bristol BS39 5RX United Kingdom

British Library Cataloguing-in-Publication Data
A catalog record for this book is available from the British Library

Thoughts on Unconventional Computing. 2021

ISBN-10: 1-905986-12-2
ISBN-13: 978-1-905986-12-5

CONTENTS

Thoughts on Unconventional Computing: Preface

There is no strict definition of unconventional computing. Being an unconventional computist is not a matter of training but thinking and living. Phenomenologically most works on unconventional computing are about implementation of computing in novel substrates (chemical, physical, biological), development of computing schemes and algorithms not fitting into the mainstream framework, or designing of computing architectures inspired by chemical or biological systems. This short book gives a snapshot of the unconventional computing field. Articles presented are punchy and well illustrated.

We don't feel there is a need to introduce each article because they all are short and self-contained and as well can be seen as extended abstracts or essays of the authors research profiles. All articles of the issue are authored by the world-leading experts in the field. The issue will serve well as a light-touch introduction to unconventional computing for people not familiar with computing and might inspire artists and humanitarians to enter the field.

Andrew Adamatzky, Bristol
Louis-José Lestocart, Paris
February 2021

Thoughts on Unconventional Computing

Photograph of the IBM Q 53 qubit quantum computer. Image courtesy of IBM.
https://newsroom.ibm.com/image-gallery-research.

Computational Nonuniversality: Philosophical and Artistic Perspectives

Selim G. Akl[1]

This paper draws connections from the science of computation to philosophy and the visual arts. The motivation for this endeavor is computational nonuniversality, a fundamental theorem in theoretical computing established relatively recently. Two distinct mathematical proofs of this result are offered, one proof by counterexample, and one proof by contradiction. Both proofs show that simulation, upon which rests the principle of universality, is not always possible, thereby making the existence of a universal computer a myth. Both proofs are inspired by philosophy of science. Both are illustrated using an artist's conception.

Introduction

The science of computation has witnessed a tremendous success since its inception in the middle of the 20th century. Today, computers are crucial in every aspect of modern society, transforming communication, transportation, education, business, health care and entertainment, to name just a few of the areas benefiting from information technology. The idea behind this extraordinary impact is a simple one, namely, *universality*. The *principle of universality* states that given sufficient time and memory space, any computation that can be performed by a general-purpose computer can, through simulation, be performed by any other general-purpose computer (regardless of any architectural differences between the simulating and simulated computers, or how efficient or inefficient is the simulation). This is accomplished by having the second computer simulate (that is, imitate exactly in order to obtain the same effect) every step executed by the first computer, using its own (hardware and software) resources. Thus, for example, an email program that runs on a laptop can be made to run equally well on a mobile phone. This applies to far more complex computations, from studying the subatomic realm to exploring the far reaches of our universe. It is indeed fair to say that simulation is the engine that would make universality possible. Consequently, according to the principle of universality, every general purpose computer is universal, capable of carrying out through simulation any computation that is possible on any other computer. And yet, it seems natural to ask: is simulation *always* possible?

In reality, the principle of universality is but a conjecture, sometimes referred to as the Church-Turing thesis. This conjecture is impossible to prove in general because an all encompassing and agreed upon definition of what constitutes a computation does not exist. This is the case, despite the overwhelming number of instances providing evidence of its validity. An abundance of examples confirming a claim is not a proof, however. By contrast, it is actually possible to *disprove* the universality conjecture, and this is precisely what this paper is about.

It was shown recently that, in fact, the principle of universality is false in general; it does not apply to all computations. The reason for this is that, as it turns out, simulation is the weakest link, the Achilles heel in the quest for universality in computation. Put simply, *simulation is not always possible*. It immediately follows that a universal computer cannot exist. This result, to which we refer as computational nonuniversality (or nonuniversality in computation) is established using two distinct approaches:

> 1. A proof by counterexample, whereby an otherwise *computable* function, cannot be computed on a putative 'universal' computer, that is, on a computer that is finite and fixed once and for all.

2. A proof by contradiction, in which it is assumed that there indeed exists a 'universal' computer, and this assumption is then shown to lead to an absurd situation whereby this computer embarks on an unending computation.

These two approaches to disproving the existence of a universal computer are reviewed in this paper. The role of philosophy in interpreting these results is highlighted. The equally important contribution of the visual arts in illustrating the proofs is put in evidence.

Nonuniversality and incompleteness

In this section we draw an analogy between Gödel's Incompleteness Theorem in mathematical logic, and the impossibility of achieving a Universal Computer in computer science, that illustrates the similarities in the formal structure and philosophical implications of the two results. Specifically, Gödel proved that there exist formal systems of mathematics that are consistent but not complete. In the same way, we show that there does not exist a general-purpose computer that is universal in the sense of being able to simulate any computation executable on another computer.

Proving nonuniversality in computation by counterexample

Let U_1 be a general-purpose computer. For the purpose of this proof, we suppose further that time is divided into discrete time units, and that U_1 is capable of $V(t)$ elementary operations at time unit number t, where t is a positive integer, $t = 1, 2, 3, \ldots$ Here, an elementary *computational* operation may be any one of the following:

1. Obtaining the value of a fixed-size variable from an external medium (for example, reading an input, measuring a physical quantity, and so on),

2. Performing an arithmetic or logical operation on a fixed number of fixed-size variables (for example, adding two numbers, comparing two numbers, and so on), and

3. Returning the value of a fixed-size variable to the outside world (for example, displaying an output, setting a physical quantity, and so on).

Each of these operations can be performed on every conceivable machine that is referred to as a *computer*. Together, they are used to define, in the most general possible way, what is meant by *to compute*: the acquisition, the transformation, and the production of information.

Now all computers today (whether theoretical or practical) have $V(t) = c$, where c is a constant (often a very large number, but still a constant). In order to make the nonuniversality result even stronger, in what follows we do not restrict $V(t)$ to be a constant. Thus, $V(t)$ is allowed to be an increasing function of time, such as $V(t) = t$, or $V(t) = 2^{2^t}$, and so on.

Finally, U_1 is allowed to have an unlimited memory in which to store its program, as well as its input data, intermediate results, and outputs. Furthermore, no limit whatsoever is placed on the time taken by U_1 to perform a computation.

Nonuniversality Theorem: U_1 cannot be a universal computer.

Proof: Let us define a computation P_1 requiring $W(t)$ operations during time unit number t, for $t = 1, 2, 3, \ldots$ If these operations are not performed by the end of time unit t, the computation P_1 is said to have failed. Let $W(t) > V(t)$, for some t. Clearly, U_1 cannot perform P_1. However, P_1 is successfully completed by another computer U_2 capable of $W(t)$ operations during the tth time unit, for $t = 1, 2, 3, \ldots$

It is important to note that, by the definition of universality, U_1, once its features have been specified, is fixed and cannot change during the computation. Despite being allowed extraordinary powers (such as, for example, the ability to increase the number of operations it can do at every consecutive time unit), U_1 still fails to perform P_1. The computer U_2 on the other hand is especially tailored to carry out P_1 and succeeds in doing so. This establishes

11

Fig. 1. Computing a function of *N* clocks.

that P_1 is definitely computable. Yet surprisingly, U_1 is unable to simulate the actions of U_2, notwithstanding the fact that no limit is placed on its memory or the time it is allowed to run. Would U_2 be the new Universal Computer? Of course not, as we can easily define a computation P_2 requiring $X(t) > W(t)$ operations during time unit t, that U_2 cannot perform. A more powerful computer U_3 can execute P_2, but is in turn defeated by a third computation P_3, and so on forever.

A pictorial example

As shown in Fig. 1, *N* clocks are hanging on a wall, $N > 1$. The clocks are digital, each displaying the time as a quadruple of digits AB:CD; for example, 19:48. All the clocks are working, ticking away synchronously. At every tick, each clock displays a new, but random, quadruple AB:CD—a time perhaps different from the ones displayed by the other $N - 1$ clocks. No clock has a memory; therefore, when at the following tick a new time is generated and displayed, the previous quadruple is lost forever. The wall is long at will, allowing *N* to be big at will. The problem to be solved is the following: For an arbitrary number of clocks *N*, it is required to compute a function (for example, the average) of the *N* times displayed at a given moment *T*. A computer capable of exactly *N* operations

per time unit, and claiming to be 'universal', readily solves the problem. It does so by reading the times displayed by the *N* clocks, and computing a function of these values all in one time unit (before time unit $T + 1$ when the clocks update their displays). This computer, however, is thwarted if even one clock is added to the wall!

An algorithmic counterexample to universality

Consider the well-known quintessential computational problem of sorting a sequence of numbers stored in the memory of a computer. For a positive even integer *n*, where $n \geq 8$, let *n* distinct integers be stored in an array *S* with *n* locations $S[1], S[2], …, S[n]$, one integer per location. Thus $S[j]$, for all $1 \leq j \leq n$, represents the integer currently stored in the jth location of *S*. In a variant of the standard sorting problem, it is required to sort the *n* integers in place into increasing order, such that:

1. After step *i* of the sorting algorithm, for all $i \geq 1$, no three consecutive integers satisfy:
   $S[j] > S[j + 1] > S[j + 2]$,
   for all $1 \leq j \leq n - 2$.

2. When the sort terminates we have:
   $S[1] < S[2] < … < S[n]$.

12

An algorithm for a computer M capable of $n/2$ operations per time unit solves the aforementioned variant of the sorting problem handily in n steps, by means of predefined pairwise swaps applied to the input array S, during each of which $S[j]$ and $S[k]$ exchange positions (using an additional memory location for temporary storage). Thus, for example, the input array

7 6 5 4 3 2 1 0

would be sorted by the following sequence of comparison/swap operations (each pair of underlined numbers are compared to one another and swapped if necessary to put the smaller first):

7 6 5 4 3 2 1 0
6 7 4 5 2 3 0 1
6 4 7 2 5 0 3 1
4 6 2 7 0 5 1 3
4 2 6 0 7 1 5 3
2 4 0 6 1 7 3 5
2 0 4 1 6 3 7 5
0 2 1 4 3 6 5 7
0 1 2 3 4 5 6 7

However, an alleged 'universal' computer capable of fewer than $(n/2)$ operations per time unit, cannot solve the problem consistently. Confronted with the input array shown above, it fails to satisfy the requirement that at no time three consecutive values are listed in decreasing order. Is M universal? Certainly not, for it too cannot solve the sorting problem when the input sequence has length greater than n.[2]

A philosophical precursor to nonuniversality

In 1931, the twenty-five year old Austrian logician Kurt Gödel published his famous Incompleteness Theorem, arguably the most important result in the history of mathematical logic. The theorem established that there exist nontrivial formal systems of mathematics that, if consistent, cannot be complete.[3]

In order to make his point, Gödel chose the formal system of simple arithmetic, that is, the natural numbers with equality, addition, and multiplication. Denoting this system by A_1, consider the following proposition G_1, expressible within A_1:

G_1 = < This statement cannot be proved within A_1 >.

Stepping outside of A_1, Gödel proved that G_1 cannot be proved within A_1. Indeed, proving it true within A_1 would mean that a false statement is true, while proving it false within A_1 would mean that a true statement is false. Since G_1 cannot be proved within A_1, it follows that G_1 is true. This means that A_1 is incomplete as it contains a true statement that cannot be proved within A_1.

To appreciate the significance of this result, consider adding the recalcitrant proposition G_1 to A_1, thus obtaining a new system A_2. Is the latter now complete? Surely not, for now we can create a proposition G_2 not provable within A_2. We can prove G_2 in a new system A_3, which in turn has its own problem proposition G_3 not provable within it, and so on forever. This result became known as Gödel's Incompleteness Theorem.

The infinite ascent of formal systems A_1, A_2, A_3, …, in the Incompleteness Theorem, is directly paralleled by the infinite ascent of aspiring 'universal' computers U_1, U_2, U_3, …, in the Nonuniversality Theorem.

It is interesting to note in passing the way in which various philosophical movements took hold of the result as a validation of their agenda. Thus, for example, to the postmodernists, Gödel's Incompleteness Theorem implied that no firm foundation exists for any system of logic. The existentialists saw in it an end to rational and objective thought. Some mathematicians and an assortment of thinkers in various disciplines argued, on the strength of the theorem, that humans are superior to machines. One physicist even suggested that, thanks to Gödel's work, it is now obvious that the human brain is not a deterministic computer; rather, it is a quantum computer.

Nonuniversality and unending recursion

Here the philosophical concept of infinite regress is used to develop a proof of nonuniversality that is distinct from the proof by counterexample. The proof itself is presented within the general framework of logic known as proof by contradiction. When invoking contradiction to prove a theorem, we begin by assuming that the claim in the theorem is false; we then show that this assumption leads logically to an absurdity (hence the Latin name *reductio ad absurdum* for this style of proof in mathematics).

Proving nonuniversality in computation by contradiction

An alternative proof of the Nonuniversality Theorem is provided in what follows.[4] Let U_1 be a general-purpose computer.

> **Nonuniversality Theorem.** U_1 cannot be a universal computer.
>
> **Proof:** Let us assume, as is commonly the case in computer science, that there exists a 'universal' computer capable of simulating any possible computation C, the latter being the result of another computer M executing a certain program on an input I. For brevity, in what follows we use M to represent both the computer as well as the program being simulated.

In order to be specific, and without any loss of generality, let the assumed 'universal' computer be U_1. We write $U_1(M, I)$ to express the fact that U_1 takes M and I as input and simulates the computation C by performing the actions of M on I. Note that U_1 is used here, by definition, as a *simulating computer*. Such a computer needs the description of another computer (M) in order to simulate *that* computer as it runs a program on its input (I). In other words, U_1 does not act directly on an input (such as I).

In what follows, let $C = (M, I)$ be a terminating computation, meaning that M runs on I and halts in a finite number of computational steps. We write $U_1[C]$ as a shorthand for $U_1(M, I)$, the simulation of C by U_1, the latter also a terminating computation.

It is evident, from the principle of universality, that the actions of U_1 itself should be possible to simulate. The question is: 'Who' is to simulate a computation performed by a universal computer? Specifically, how are the actions of U_1–as it simulates C, that is, $U_1[C]$–*themselves* to be simulated?

There are two options.

> **Option 1.** U_1 simulates itself. We write $U_1[U_1[C]]$ to indicate that U_1 is simulating $U_1[C]$. This means that U_1 is executing the actions of itself (U_1, the computer), on the simulation ($U_1[C]$, the input); we write:
>
> $$U_1[U_1[C]] = U_1(U_1, U_1[C]).$$
>
> The right hand side of the above expression, has three U_1s: the first is the simulator, the second is the computer being simulated, and the third, $U_1[C]$, is the input. We therefore have:
>
> $$\begin{aligned} U_1[U_1[C]] &= U_1(U_1, U_1[C]) \\ &= U_1(U_1[U_1[C]]) \\ &= U_1(U_1(U_1, U_1[C])) \\ &= U_1(U_1(U_1[U_1[C]])) \\ &= U_1(U_1(U_1(U_1, U_1[C]))) \end{aligned}$$
> $$\dots$$
>
> This leads to a *self-referential* infinite regress, with U_1 simulating itself, simulating itself, simulating itself,… The computation just described is a non-terminating process (one could say that it is not even a computation, by definition, since it does not halt, but that is not important for our purpose). It follows that U_1 has failed to simulate itself, while executing a *terminating* computation C.

> **Option 2.** We can stipulate the existence of a more powerful universal computer U_2 that simulates $U_1[C]$. Again, this leads, in turn, to an *ascending* infinite regress, featuring a sequence of ever more powerful computers $U_2, U_3, U_4, \dots, U_n, U_{n+1}, U_{n+2}, \dots$, performing simulations $C_1, C_2, C_3, \dots, C_n, C_{n+1}, C_{n+2} \dots$
>
> Formally,
> $$\begin{aligned} C_1 &= U_2[U_1[C]], \\ C_2 &= U_3[U_2[U_1[C]]], \\ C_3 &= U_4[U_3[U_2[U_1[C]]]], \\ &\dots \end{aligned}$$
> $$C_{n+1} = U_{n+2}[U_{n+1} \dots U_4[U_3[U_2[U_1[C]]]]\dots],$$
> $$\dots$$
>
> and so on *ad infinitum*. In the unending sequence of computations described here, computer U_{n+1} is needed to simulate U_n, for $n = 1, 2, 3, \dots$, given that computer U_n cannot simulate itself (as shown in Option 1 for U_1).

Both Option 1 and Option 2 are computationally absurd, leading to one conclusion:

Fig. 2. Self reference and unending recursion.

the assumption regarding the existence of a universal computer U_1 is false. No computer is universal.

Absolute idealism and self-referential cartography

As the sun was setting on the 19th century, idealist philosopher Josiah Royce proposed an interesting thought experiment. Imagine, he suggested, we could draw a detailed map of England. The map would be so precise as to contain every road, every river, every hill, every plain, and so on. A flat terrain will be chosen and the map inscribed on the surface of the English countryside. But then something unexpected would happen. Since the map is now part of the landscape, in order for it to be exact, it would necessarily have to contain a copy of itself. That copy would therefore inevitably contain a copy of itself as well, and the copy of the copy a copy, …; the process will continue indefinitely. This self-referential map-within-a map construction is known as the map of England problem and is sometimes used in studies of consciousness.[5] A whimsical illustration of self-reference and the potential for infinite regress is shown in Fig. 2.

Conclusion

On a hot August day in the year 1900, the illustrious German mathematician David Hilbert addressed the International Congress of Mathematicians assembled at the Sorbonne in Paris. Hilbert presented his colleagues with a list of problems on which, he believed, they should spend their time in the new century. Among these problems was the question of whether there exists a fixed set of true mathematical statements that can be used to prove *automatically* any new mathematical statement. Hilbert's objective was the formalization of mathematics.

The purpose of Hilbert's program in formalizing mathematics was twofold. The first goal was to contain infinity. Proofs for all true statements of a formal system were to be produced from a finite set of axioms. The second goal was to eliminate intuition from mathematics. By mechanizing proof generation, serendipity would no longer be part of the process of doing mathematics. Gödel's work demonstrated that, on the contrary, infinity is an integral part of mathematics and cannot be tamed. Mathematicians will always use their intuition to reason about the infinite.

Likewise, the Nonuniversality Theorem shows that no finite computer can be universal. A new machine will always be needed to cope with the next challenge. The resemblance between the Nonuniversality Theorem and the Incompleteness Theorem is captured by the

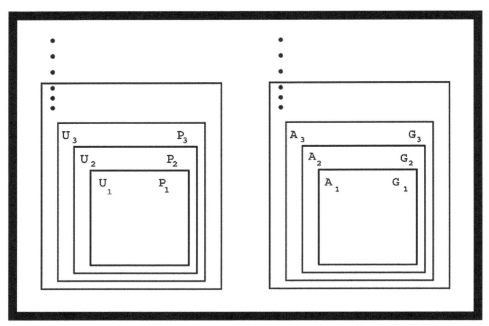

Fig. 3. Nonuniversality and incompleteness.

drawing in Fig. 3. For every computer thought to be universal, there exists a computational problem that it cannot solve, even if given unbounded time and space; a more powerful computer is required. Similarly, for every set of axioms thought to be complete, there exists a proposition that it cannot prove; an augmented set of axioms is required.

The idea of nonuniversality in computation is not a new one. Several proofs *by counterexample* of the non-existence of a universal computer have been presented since early in this century. They described different unconventional computational paradigms that falsify the idea of a universal computer. Examples of such paradigms include computations with: time varying variables, time varying computational complexity, rank varying computational complexity, interacting variables, uncertain time constraints, mathematical constraints, global variables, and so on. These computational problems imply that computation is a fundamental category of Nature, and as such it has no bounds. Its parameters are limitless. Time passes, inexorably, changing everything in its path. The constituents of our physical space constantly interact with one another, mutually affecting each other. As our world evolves,

computations are taking place everywhere, all the time. The genie simply does not fit in the bottle.

By contrast with the proof by counterexample, the proof of nonuniversality in computation *by contradiction* is a more recent result. It was motivated when an obvious and logical question was asked, apparently for the first time ever: If simulation is the bedrock of computing, and the supposed 'universal' computer can simulate any computation, how can the actions of the 'universal' computer *itself* be simulated? The answer led once again to the collapse of the notion of universality. This, in turn, leads here to the following interesting observation. The invention in 1899 of the self-referential map-of-England metaphor, bringing about an inevitable infinite regress along with it, predates by 121 years the discovery of a proof, by self-simulation, of computational nonuniversality. Miraculously, the former (old result) serves as a striking illustration of the latter (new result), as demonstrated in Fig. 4.

We note in closing that nonuniversality in computation applies to all known computational models and existing conventional computers, both sequential and parallel, as well as applying to all future unconventional computers, including quantum computers, biomolecular

16

Fig. 4. Self-simulation and the ensuing infinite regress.

computers, chemical computers, and so on. Like the Halting Problem in Computer Science, Incompleteness in Mathematics, and the Uncertainty Principle in Physics, Nonuniversality in Computation is a limiting theorem, an impossibility result.

I am grateful to my daughter Sophia for the beautiful drawings in this paper.

[1] School of Computing, Queen's University, Kingston, Ontario K7L 3N6, Canada, akl@cs.queensu.ca.
[2] S. G. AKL, "Unconventional computational problems," in R. A. MEYERS (ed.), *Encyclopedia of Complexity and Systems Science*, New York, Springer, 2018, 631-639.
[3] K. GÖDEL, "Über formal unentscheidbare Sätze der Principia Mathematica und verwandter Systeme I," *Monatshefte für Methematik und Physik 38*, 1931, 173-198.
[4] S. G. AKL, "A map of England, the simulator simulated, and nonuniversality in computation," to appear in: *International Journal of Unconventional Computing*.
[5] J. ROYCE, *The World and The Individual, First Series: The Four Historical Conceptions of Being*, New York, Dover Publications, 1959, 504-505.

Swarms of microscopic agents self-assemble into complex bodies

Bruce MacLennan[1]

Nature produces living bodies of magnificent beauty and complexity, which are not the work of an external artist, but of a self-organized dance of a vast number of microscopic cells communicating and coordinating with each other. We can learn the dance scores from nature and use them to control massive swarms of microscopic artificial agents to assemble complex structures organized at many hierarchical levels, from the nanoscale up to the macroscale. Simulations demonstrate the application of these ideas in artificial intelligence and artificial life.

The Problem

As Richard Feynman said, "there is plenty of room at the bottom,"[2] and we are discovering ways to organize matter and processes at the microscopic scale — and even at the nanoscale — that have macroscopic effects that are relevant to technology, medicine, and art. But to date, nanotechnology has been limited to the creation of simple structures with a relatively small number of components, or to structures with a large number of components with either a highly regular or a random organization. For many purposes, however, we need to be able to create complex structures hierarchically organized at many spatial scales from the microscopic to the macroscopic. Consider these examples.

The contemporary, most successful approaches to artificial intelligence are inspired by the brain; they strive to model massive neural networks at a level of abstraction that preserves their information processing capabilities while omitting irrelevant biological detail. Research in cognitive neuroscience and artificial neural networks has revealed that much of the flexible, context-sensitive information processing of our brains depends on large numbers of massively interconnected neurons (9×10^{10} neurons in a human brain, with perhaps 10^{15} connections). Moreover, these neurons are not arranged and interconnected in either a regular or a random pattern; there are complex organizations both within individual brain regions and among the regions. All this within a volume of 1100 to 1300 cm³, and consuming about 20W of power. If we want to achieve human-scale artificial intelligence, it is reasonable to suppose that we may need to construct artificial brains similarly organized from the microscale to the macroscale (Fig. 1).

Continuing the example of artificial intelligence, we now understand much better the importance of embodiment as a foundation for intelligence.[3] Brains have evolved to control physical bodies in their physical environments, although, of course, we also use them for abstract thought and contemplation. Nevertheless, control of our mechanically complex bodies by means of rich sensorimotor feedback provides the foundation from which language and abstract thought can emerge. Large numbers of sensory neurons embedded in our muscles, joints, and skin provide rich, high-dimensional input that allows our (quite slow) neurons to coordinate complex behavior in real time. Future robots with physical competence comparable to that of animals will be facilitated by similarly complex artificial sense organs, skin, and muscles (actuators). Although macroscopic in size, they will be complex structures of many microscopic parts. For example, the human eye has approximately 100 million retinal cells, which preprocess the visual image in real time, reducing its dimension so that it can be transmitted on about one million optic nerve fibers. It is not unreasonable to suppose that an artificial eye, with similar visual acuity and information processing capacity to ours, will have similar complexity. Such robotic devices will have important

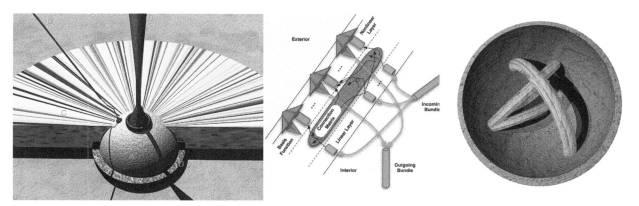

Fig. 1. Depictions of large-scale neurocomputer.[4] To left, external connections to artificial cortex. In center, computational microstructure of artificial cortex. To right, example of three massive fiber bundles connecting functional regions of cortex.

applications in medicine, such as prosthetic limbs and sense organs. Surely, we would like prosthetic eyes with the sensitivity and acuity of natural eyes, and prosthetic hands with the dexterity and sense of touch of natural hands, but these require vast numbers of components to be assembled in precise ways.

Artificial Morphogenesis

Assembling many millions of components into complex systems, structured from the nanoscale up through the macroscale, might seem impossible, but developmental processes in embryos prove that it is possible. An embryo develops from a single cell, which divides repeatedly producing an exponentially growing cell mass. These cells differentiate and orchestrate a complex dance that assembles the tissues, organs, and limbs of a complete organism (3.7×10^{13} cells in a human adult). A foetus may comprise a trillion cells, which have self-organized into innumerable structures at many spatial scales spanning five orders of magnitude. In this robust process, cells migrate, following chemical waystations to distant destinations, signaling each other to coordinate their movement and trigger context-sensitive differentiation into hundreds of cell types. Masses of cells flow viscously, forming intricately structured tissues that stretch, fold, and grow. This is our inspiration.

Artificial morphogenesis applies the principles of embryological morphogenesis to coordinating very large numbers of simple agents to assemble complex hierarchical structures.[5] It

may be considered one approach to *morphogenetic engineering*, which applies principles of morphogenesis to the creation of form.[6] In artificial morphogenesis, very large numbers of microscopic agents cooperate to assemble themselves and inanimate microscopic components into a desired structure (Fig. 2). Under some conditions, they can disassemble such a structure in order to reassemble it into a new form.

The agents, which may be wholly artificial or produced by synthetic biology, have relatively simple capabilities for motion, signaling, and information processing and control. Agents need to be able to signal their immediate neighbors, but also more distant agents in order to coordinate their behavior. Cells in a developing embryo accomplish this by emitting chemical morphogens, which diffuse in the intercellular environment and can be detected by other cells. Likewise, in artificial morphogenesis, agents communicate by chemical and other signals. Agents also need to be able to move, either through a fluid medium or as a viscoelastic mass. This movement is accomplished by a variety of simple mechanical mechanisms. Finally, the behavior of agents is governed by relatively simple, primarily analog control mechanisms.

Progress in microrobotics is ongoing, and we anticipate that there will soon be sub-millimeter-scale autonomous robots with the capabilities required for artificial morphogenesis. Another attractive option is to use the techniques of synthetic biology to modify microorganisms

19

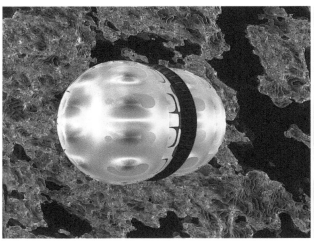

Fig. 2. Artistic depiction of microrobots. To the left, a single microrobot attached to a surface.
To the right, a swarm of microrobots assembling into a layer of an artificial tissue.

to implement the required agents. Genetic regulatory circuits are essentially analog control mechanisms, and they can be modified to implement the behavior required of a morphogenetic agent. Another advantage of biological agents is that they can reproduce, thus eliminating the need to manufacture artificial agents in large numbers.

Agents move in coordinated masses and differentiate under the influence of signaling substances that diffuse in the environment. Since our goal is to have very large numbers of very small agents moving *en masse*, we describe morphogenetic processes by partial differential equations (PDEs), which treats the agent mass as a continuous fluid or tissue. Embryologists often use PDEs for the same reason, and we can use their equations in artificial morphogenesis. Mathematically, we treat our agents as infinitesimal particles moving under the influence of forces and morphogen concentrations. This approach helps to ensure that our algorithms scale up to very large numbers of very small agents, but also keeps them largely scale-invariant, that is, independent of the exact size of the agents relative to the macroscopic object being constructed.

Examples

Since the required microscopic agents are not yet available, we test our morphogenetic algorithms through simulation.[7]

Our first example (Fig. 3) shows how an indefinite but very large number of agents can be coordinated to lay down neural fiber bundles between selected regions of an artificial brain.[8] In this morphogenetic algorithm the bundles are grown one at a time. A massive swarm of agents (equal in number to the number of nerve fibers in the bundle) is injected at the origin region, and they follow the gradient of a morphogen diffusing from the destination region, depositing fiber material as they go. Once a bundle has been created, its material absorbs the attractant, and this causes agents to steer around already created bundles, avoiding collisions. Moreover we can allow fiber bundles to split to go around obstacles when that is required.

Our second example (Fig. 4) shows how natural morphogenetic processes —in this case spinal segmentation — can be used for both similar and different applications in artificial morphogenesis, in this case, assembling an insect-like robot body frame.[9] The example exploits the idea that in morphogenesis, patterns in time can create patterns in space. In this case we use the clock-and-wavefront model of spinal segmentation, which was first proposed in 1976 but finally confirmed in 2008.[10] We use this process to assemble the spine of a robot, which is similar to its function in vertebrate development, but we also use it to assemble segmented legs, which develop differently in nature. Thus we are using a natural process both for a purpose that it served in nature (spinal segmentation) and also for a purpose it does not serve in nature (leg segmentation). The number and lengths of the segments are parameters that we can control in each case.

In brief, morphogenesis proceeds as follows. Agents are recruited to assemble between the spine and the tail bud, which is moved rightward. Both the tail bud and completed spinal segments produce morphogens which diffuse into the undifferentiated spinal region. Periodically (and this is the temporal patterning),

a pacemaker in the tail bud produces a pulse of a third morphogen, which is propagated through the tissue toward the head. As it passes through a region of relatively low concentrations of the first two morphogens, it leads to differentiation of a new spinal segment. The length of the segments is determined by the ratio of the growth rate and the pacemaker frequency; the number of segments is controlled by the product of pacemaker frequency and the growth time. This same process is used to grow segmented legs on the spinal segments.

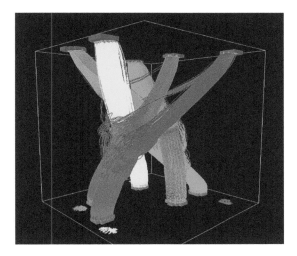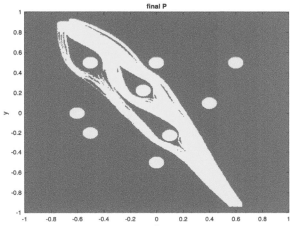

Fig. 3. To the left, simulation of swarms of 5000 agents depositing neural fiber bundles between randomly chosen origins and destinations. To the right, simulation of massive swarm of agents creating paths around obstacles from lower right to upper left.

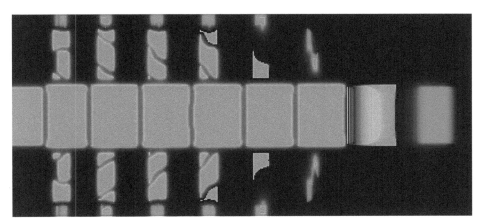

Fig. 4. Simulation of assembly of insect-like robot body frame using clock-and-wavefront process. Head end to left, tail end to right. Red color denotes wave of segmentation morphogen propagating to left, which has just passed through and differentiated the right-most tan segment. Similar processes are simultaneously assembling and differentiating leg segments.

Conclusions

Morphogenetic processes in nature can be imitated and adapted to control massive swarms of microscopic agents to assemble complex, hierarchically structured systems. Describing these processes by partial differential equations describing masses of infinitesimal particles helps to ensure that they scale up to very large numbers of microscopic agents, which is what will be required for the self-assembly of very complex structures, organized from the microscale up to the macroscale. In this way, we may hope to produce artifacts of a similar sophistication to those in nature.

[1] Associate Professor Emeritus, Department of Electrical Engineering & Computer Science, University of Tennessee.

[2] R. P. FEYNMAN, "There's plenty of room at the bottom," *Engineering and Science 23*, 1960, 22-36. https://resolver.caltech.edu/CaltechES:23.5.1960Bottom

[3] See, for example, A. CLARK, *Being There: Putting Brain, Body, and World Together Again*, Cambridge, MIT Press, 1997, and G. LAKOFF, M. JOHNSON, *Philosophy in the Flesh: The Embodied Mind and its Challenge to Western Thought*, New York, Basic Books, 1999.

[4] B. J. MACLENNAN, "The U-machine: A model of generalized computation," *International Journal of Unconventional Computing 6*, 2010, 265-283.

[5] On artificial morphogenesis, see for example B. J. MACLENNAN, "Morphogenesis as a model for nano communication," *Nano Communication Networks 1*, 2010, 199-208, and B. J. MACLENNAN, "The morphogenetic path to programmable matter," *Proceedings of the IEEE 103*, 2015, 1226-1232.

[6] On morphogenetic engineering, see for example R. DOURSAT, H. SAYAMA, O. MICHEL, "A review of morphogenetic engineering," *Natural Computing 12*, 2013, 517-535, and H. OH, A. R. SHIRAZI, C. SUN, Y. JIN, "Bio-inspired self-organising multi-robot pattern formation: A review," *Robotics and Autonomous Systems 91*, 2017, 83-100.

[7] B. J. MACLENNAN, A. C. MCBRIDE, "Swarm intelligence for morphogenetic engineering," in A. SCHUMANN (ed.), *Swarm Intelligence: From Social Bacteria to Human Beings*, Boca Raton, Taylor & Francis / CRC, 2020, 9-54.

[8] B. J. MACLENNAN, "A morphogenetic program for path formation by continuous flocking," *International Journal of Unconventional Computing 14*, 2019, 91-119.

[9] B. J. MACLENNAN, "Coordinating swarms of microscopic agents to assemble complex structures," in Y. TAN (ed.), *Swarm Intelligence, Vol. 1: Principles, Current Algorithms and Methods*, PBCE 119, Institution of Engineering and Technology, 2018, Chap. 20, 583-612.

[10] J. COOKE, E. C. ZEEMAN, "A clock and wavefront model for control of the number of repeated structures during animal morphogenesis," *Journal of Theoretical Biology 58*, 1976, 455-476. M.-L. DEQUÉANT, O. POURQUIÉ, "Segmental patterning of the vertebrate embryonic axis," *Nature Reviews Genetics 9*, 2008, 370-382.

Exploring chaos with analog computers

Bernd Ulmann[1]

This article shows how chaotic systems and their behaviour can be explored using analog computers instead of the now prevalent digital approach.

Many natural systems, even very simple ones such as a damped pendulum with an external driving force exhibit chaotic behaviour. One of the main characteristics of such systems is their extreme sensitivity to changes in initial conditions, something often called the "Butterfly Effect." Although these systems are fully deterministic and thus can be described mathematically in closed form, which implies that their future behaviour is completely determined by their past and thus their initial conditions, they are nonetheless not predictable. The term "chaos" was characterised by Edward Norton Lorenz, one of the founders of modern chaos theory, as follows: *"Chaos: When the present determines the future, but the approximate present does not approximately determine the future."*[2] Interestingly, Lorenz did his groundbreaking work on a tiny digital computer, a Royal McBee LGP-30[3] which is only marginally suited for exploring chaotic systems at best.

To introduce the idea of an analog computer, a short recapitulation of the basic operation of a stored-program digital computer might help: A modern digital computer (typically) has a fixed internal structure, *i.e.* there are one or more arithmetic logic units (ALU), there is a central memory system (nowadays supplemented by a hierarchy of cache memory subsystems to speed things up), and there is a central control unit in addition to a number of input/output channels, *etc.* All of this is controlled by means of a stream of instructions, an "algorithm," stored in memory. At every moment such a machine executes one or more instructions from memory and may decide which instruction to read and process in the next step based on the result of prior instructions executed. So the execution of a program on such a digital computer is basically strictly sequential. (There are, of course, parallel digital computers but exploring this parallelism and achieving a high degree of parallelism is typically at least difficult and most problems won't scale well with this respect.)

In contrast to this, an analog computer has no fixed internal structure, it even has no memory at all and is not programmed by a sequence of instruction to be executed. At its heart an analog computer consists of a number of computing elements, each of which implements a basic operation such as summation, integration, multiplication, *etc.* Values are typically represented in a (basically) continuous form as voltages or currents and not as sequences of bits. (There are, indeed, "digital analog computers," so-called "Digital Differential Analysers," DDAs for short, but these are outside the scope of this article.) Programming an analog computer means to devise a scheme by which the various computing elements are interconnected in order to form a "model," an "analogue" for the problem to be solved.

Although analog computers have been largely forgotten for the last decades due to the low price and ubiquity of stored program digital computers, they have some advantages over their digital rivals, most notably they are extremely energy efficient (in most modern applications for analog computers this high degree of energy efficiency will be the main driver for their application), they interface well to our analog world, and they are inherently interactive. This interactivity is one of the key advantages when it comes to the study of dynamic systems in general and chaotic systems in special, where a researcher can easily change some parameters and "see" the effect in realtime on some output device such as an oscilloscope.[4]

Figure 1 shows a modern analog computer, an Analog Paradigm Model-1 in its basic configuration. The top chassis contains (among power supplies) four comparators which can be used to model discontinuities, eight manual precision potentiometers which can be used to set coefficients and initial conditions for a simulation, and a manual control unit which allows the machine to operate either in a manual mode where its operation is controlled by a human operator, or in repetitive-mode where one simulation run is repeated over and over again at (typically) high speed in order to get a flicker free picture on an oscilloscope screen. The lower chassis contains eight multipliers, eight summers, and four integrators. (This is part of the real "magic" of an analog computer – integration is one of its basic functions!)

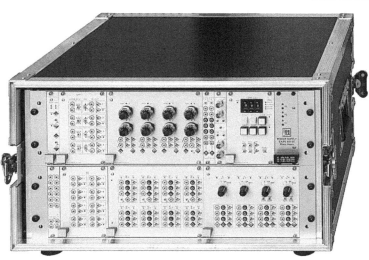

Fig. 1. Small scale analog computer.

Mathematically, dynamic systems can be described by so-called differential equations (DEQ for short), i.e. equations in which the unknown is not a value (this would be typically quite simple to solve) but instead a time-varying function. Such DEQs are the tool of choice when it comes to modelling natural systems and are notoriously hard to solve, in fact most differential equations have no analytical solution, i.e. there is no closed mathematical expression describing the solution to such an equation. Thus the only viable way to gain an understanding of the underlying system is by means of simulation, be it digital or analog.

Figure 2 shows part of a typical analog computer setup. What looks like an intricate maze of wires is the actual program (at least part of it as the overall program spans many more computing elements) which directly resembles the mathematical problem being solved. This is in contrast to a stored-program digital computer where the underlying mathematical problem has to be translated into a suitable algorithm yielding the desired solution. This additional and often rather error prone and convoluted step can be skipped altogether with an analog computer, the mathematical formulation of a problem is basically sufficient to program an analog computer (sans scaling, which is out of scope here as well).

One of the simplest systems exhibiting chaotic behaviour is a damped pendulum such as a swing being exhibited to an external driving force that might be of a harmonic nature in the most general case. The behaviour of this oscillatory system can then be represented by a "phase space plot," i.e. a graphical description of the time-dependent variation of two or more variables involved in the problem. In the case of a pendulum, its angle, the angular velocity, and the angular acceleration could be of interest. Typically, the angular velocity and acceleration are used as x- and y-coordinates for the phase-space plot describing

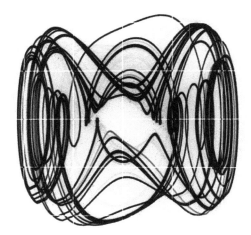

Fig. 3. Phase space plot of a damped pendulum exhibited to an external force.

the behaviour of the system, as shown in the following figure. The chaotic nature of the pendulum's movement can be easily seen.

A figure like in figure 3 is called an "attractor", which is basically a subset of a phase space, *i.e.* a set of values a dynamic system will finally evolve to.

Performing a simulation like this on an analog computer has the advantage that changes in parameters such as the damping or the excitation frequency, *etc.*, can be performed manually by setting potentiometers during run time. This allows one to gain a real "feel" of the behaviour of complex systems as parameter changes take immediate effect and can be directly observed on an oscilloscope.

The next example is the already mentioned original chaotic system first described by Lorenz, a result of early research in atmospheric sciences. He discovered the chaotic nature of this problem through simulations on a digital computer, which was slow and tedious back then. (It is not clear as of now why he did not use an analog computer for his research as the advantages would have been even more profound in his days than they are now.) The system treated by Lorenz is described by three coupled differential equations and represents a simplified model for atmospheric convection.

The three equations involved are parameterised by three coefficients. The original parameter set yields the attractor shown in figure 4.

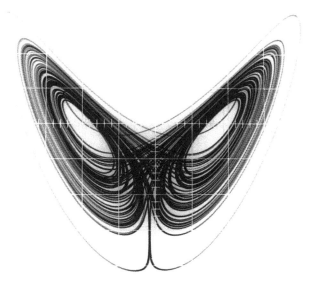

Fig. 4. Typical display of the Lorenz attractor.

This so-called "Lorenz attractor" is a special form of an attractor as it is a "strange attractor," *i.e.* it exhibits a fractal structure. The state of the system at every point in time can be characterised by its corresponding point on this (rather beautiful) graph. The interesting thing is that even tiniest deviations in the initial conditions will lead the system to points far apart on the attractor, so it is not possible to predict the future behaviour of the system. On the other hand, the system cannot "leave" its attractor (at least not for its parameters and initial values within suitable intervals), so the attractor faithfully describes the system behaviour without the chance of actually predicting it from measurements or the like.

All in all, electronic analog computers are ideal tools to explore the behaviour of chaotic (and other dynamic) systems and modern developments in this field will lead to highly integrated analog computers, which will form hybrid computers when combined with classic digital computers thus bringing the advantages of analog computing to a rather wide audience.

[1] Professor for business informatics at the "Hochschule für Oekonomie und Management" in Frankfurt/Main, Germany, and a guest professor and lecturer at the Institute of Medical Systems Biology at Ulm University, ulmann@analogparadigm.com. A number of application notes, including the chaotic systems described here can be found at http://analogparadigm.com/documentation.html, and the author is happy to answer your questions on analog computing.

[2] C. M. DANFORTH, "Chaos in an Atmosphere Hanging on a Wall," on line: http://mpe.dimacs.rutgers.edu/2013/03/17/chaos-in-an-atmosphere-hanging-on-a-wall/

[3] E. N. LORENZ, "Deterministic Nonperiodic Flow," *Journal of the the Atmospheric Sciences 20*, 1963, 130-141.

[4] For more background information and the history of analog computers, see B. ULMANN, *Analog Computing*, München, De Gruyter Oldenbourg, 2013.

Are There Traces of Megacomputing in Our Universe

Olga Kosheleva and Vladik Kreinovich[1]

The recent successes of quantum computing encouraged many researchers to search for other unconventional physical phenomena that could potentially speed up computations. Several promising schemes have been proposed that will – hopefully – lead to faster computations in the future. Some of these schemes – similarly to quantum computing – involve using events from the micro-world while others involve using large-scale phenomena. If some civilization used micro-world for computations, this will be difficult for us to notice, but if they use mega-scale effects, maybe we can notice these phenomena? In this paper, we analyze what possible traces such megacomputing can leave – and come up with rather surprising conclusions.

Modern computers are fast. By performing billions of computational steps, we can reasonably well predict tomorrow's weather – and when the prediction is not perfect, the problem is usually not with the computers, but with the fact that we do not have enough weather-related sensors in many geographic areas. Onboard computers allow missiles to fly close to the ground at astronomical speeds without hitting the ground. A recent quarantine enables billions of people to be connected by reasonably reliable video-connection, helping many people continue to work, to study, and even to enjoy (remotely) their favorite operas.

But for many practical applications, computers are still too slow. For example, a large part of the US is threatened by destructive tornadoes, and we still do not have a reliable means to predict where a tornado will be moving. As a result, in tornado-prone areas, alarms sound so often – and usually, with no actual tornado coming – that when the actual deadly tornado comes, people do not react to the warning, do not evacuate – and the consequences may be disastrous. Here, we know the equations that would describe the tornado's dynamics – they are largely the same equations that allow us to predict tomorrow's weather. Experiments have shown that by spending the same computation time (several hours) on a supercomputer, we can predict where a tornado will go in the next 15 minutes – but that is too late. This is just one example, there are many other problems like

that. Many of such problems are related to organic chemistry and biochemistry. So it is not surprising that, *e.g.* in our university, the main users of high-performance computers are not – as one may think – computer scientists, but folks from the Department of Chemistry and Biochemistry.

How can we make computers faster? Journalists writing about science often express an optimistic belief that human ingenuity will solve all the problems. We are optimistic too, but with computers, we cannot be to optimistic: we are currently reaching the bounds set by fundamental physics. This bound is very simple to explain. According to modern physics, nothing can travel faster that the speed of light – *i.e.* faster than 300 000 km/sec, or 300 000 000 m/sec. How does this affect computations? A usual laptop of which we are typing this article is about 30 cm in diameter, *i.e.* 0.3 m. This means that for a signal to go from one side of the computer to another, we need 0.3/300 000 000 sec, *i.e.* 0.000 000 001 seconds. This may sound like a very small time, but even on the cheapest 4 GigaHerz computer, the processor can perform 4 operations while a signal is still travelling.

To make computers faster, we need to shrink their processing elements even more – this is why we enter the realm of quantum computing.[2] But there is a limit to this shrinkage. Already, a processing element may consist of a few thousand atoms. We can theoretically shrink more, to the level of a single atom – but then what? Then we are stuck.

So what can we do? In this long-term prospective, quantum physics does not seem to help, so let us look at other possible physical phenomena. It would help if we could find a way to speed up all the processes – that will speed up computations as well. Unfortunately, in modern physics, there is no known way to speed up all the processes – there are only ways to slow them down.

According to Einstein's Special Relativity Theory,[3] processes slow down when we travel with a speed close to the speed of light. Actually, they also slow down when we fly on a plane, but that slow-down is so miniscule that often super-precise clocks can detect it, while for the particles in a particle accelerator (that move practically at speed of light), the time slows down so much that their average decay time increases by orders of magnitude.

According to General Relativity Theory,[4] processes also slow down when we are in a strong gravitational field – e.g. near a massive black hole. Yes, they also slow done when a usual gravitational field becomes a little stronger, but this change is also minuscule.

Is the situation hopeless? Good news is that, by the very name of relativity theory, many things are relative. There is no absolute time with respect to which we want computers to be faster, all we want is that the computers be faster with respect to our time. In other words, what we want is to make sure that computers are in one environment, and we are in another environment, and all the processes in the computer-containing environment should be much faster than all the processes in our environment. We cannot achieve this by staying on Earth and placing computers somewhere else – the only thing we would then achieve is that, in comparison to our time, computers will be even slower than they are now. But what we can do is leave computers where they are – and place ourselves in situations where time will go slower. If we manage to slow down our own time by a factor of ten, then the same problem that requires five hours of computation in computer-time will feel like half an

hour for us – and this is exactly what we want. In other words, instead of speeding up computers, we can slow down ourselves, our whole civilization. How can we do it? As we mentioned, there are two ways to do it: we can start travelling with a speed close to the speed of light, and/or we can place ourselves in a strong gravitational field. Let us consider these two options one by one, starting with fast travel.[5]

We cannot immediately go from 0 to 300 000 km/sec: we can only survive the acceleration similar to the Earth's gravitational acceleration of 9.81 m/sec^2. So we need to start going slowly. We cannot travel on the same orbit around the Sun – if we start travelling with too high a speed, centrifugal forces will squeeze us, so we need to go further and further away from the Sun. We cannot simply travel away on a straight line – this way, we will reach a high speed, but by that time, we will be so far away from the left-behind computers that communication time will eat up all the advantages. So the only way to reach the desired effect is to make circles which are becoming wider and wider – in other words, to follow a spiral trajectory.

This acceleration requires a lot of energy. Where can we get this energy? We have to get it as we travel, from the interplanetary and then interstellar particles and gases – and other objects. As we follow this spiral trajectory, we will burn whatever we can, leaving practically nothing. So what will remain? What will remain is empty spaces forming a spiral. Sounds familiar? It should: this is exactly how our own Galaxy and many other galaxies look like.

So maybe the spiral shape of our Galaxy is indeed the trace of an ancient megacomputing civilization? But wait, there is more.

As we have mentioned, another way to speed up is to place oneself in a strong gravitational field – e.g. near a massive black hole. At first, we can use existing black holes, but what if we want to perform even faster computations? The only way to do that is to make the black hole bigger and bigger – thus increasing its gravitational field and slowing us down even more. So how will be known that a supercivilization used this idea to perform megacomputations?

28

By observing a humongous black hole that our previous astrophysical theories did not explain.

Sounds familiar? It should. According to modern astrophysics, there is indeed a very massive black hole in the center of our Galaxy – and in the centers of many other galaxies. So maybe these black holes are also traces of megacomputing civilizations?

Who knows?

This work was supported in part by the US National Science Foundation grants 1623190 (A Model of Change for Preparing a New Generation for Professional Practice in Computer Science) and HRD-1242122 (Cyber-ShARE Center of Excellence).

[1] Olga Kosheleva and Vladik Kreinovich, University of Texas at El Paso, El Paso, TX 79968, USA, olgak@utep.edu, vladik@utep.edu

[2] See for instance M. A. NIELSEN & I. L. CHUANG, *Quantum Computation and Quantum Information*, Cambridge, Cambridge University Press, 2000.

[3] See for instance R. FEYNMAN, R. LEIGHTON, and M. SANDS, *The Feynman Lectures on Physics*, Boston, Addison Wesley, 2005, and K. S. THORNE & R. D. BLANDFORD, *Modern Classical Physics: Optics, Fluids, Plasmas, Elasticity, Relativity, and Statistical Physics*, Princeton, Princeton University Press, 2017.

[4] See *ibidem*.

[5] Readers interested in technical details can look into O. KOSHELEVA & V. KREINOVICH, "Relativistic effects can be used to achieve a universal square-root (or even faster) computation speedup," in A. BLASS, P. CEGIELSKY, N. DERSHOWITZ, M. DROSTE, and B. FINKBEINER (eds.), *Fields of Logic and Computation III*, Springer, to appear.

An example of a spiral galaxy, the Pinwheel Galaxy (also known as Messier 101 or NGC 5457).

Communication, information and music

Dawid Przyczyna,[1] Marcin Strzelecki,[2] Konrad Szaciłowski[3]

In this brief article, we would like to take the reader on a journey through the fields of information, communication and music, as well as the places where these domains intersect. As it turns out, contemporary and seemingly abstract concepts related to information processing can be conveyed in an accessible form through music. To spice things up, the thoughts in this article are supplemented with pictures of postage stamps, which include all of the above-mentioned concepts.

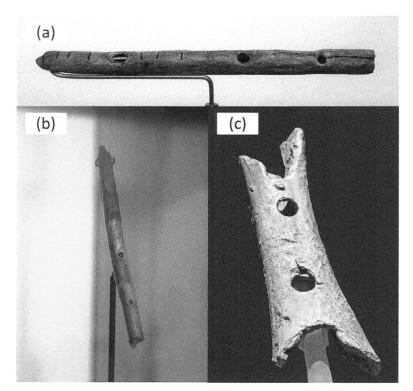

Fig. 1. Paleolithic musical instruments: upper Paleolithic from Geissenklösterle (a), middle Paleolithic flute, ca. 35000-40000 years, (b) and neandertalic flute from Divje Babe Cave (Slovenia, 55000 years ago, c).
Photos courtesy José-Manuel Benito (a), Marco Ciamella (b) and Jean-Pierre Dalbéra (c).

Communication between organisms is an ubiquitous phenomenon, both at intraspecies and interspecies level in all kingdoms: *Archaea*, *Bacteria*, *Protista*, *Fungi*, *Plantae* and *Animalia*. Surprisingly, primitive communication was detected even between individual virions. All these organisms possess both intracellular, intraorganismic and transorganismic communication protocols, however the most complex and interesting ones, from the point of view of information theory, are those between individual organisms. In most cases the intracellular and intraorganismic communication is based on signalling molecules, the same concerns most of the interorganismic and interspecies communication protocols. Communication in general can be described as a sign-mediated interaction between at least two living entities, which share the common repertoire of signs representing a form of natural language. These signs may be combined according to syntactic rules in various contexts (according to pragmatic rules) and used to transport biologically relevant information. Almost all kingdoms of life use molecules as the only available communication tool, whereas animals add vocal and visual communication tools to their repertoire of available signs.

In humans, these evolutionary novelties dominate, almost completely, over the molecular language, however "molecular senses" of olfaction and gustation are still significantly important. Most of animals use senses of vision and hearing for most of their communication purposes. Whereas our own (human) senses seem to be impaired (as compared with some predatory birds), their ability to process signals is still amazing. We have also developed unique ways of communication: music and language, manifested sonically as speech, and graphically as writing. These tools provide an unprecedented opportunity to communicate language and emotions using graphical symbols and aesthetic, religious and cultural feelings via organized sounds of different parameters like pitch, durations, and timbral qualities, arranged in melodic, rhythmic, and harmonic (tonal) patterns.

Music is the only form of natural communication, that is created and perceived only by humans (however studies on animals indicate some aspects of sensitivity to music). Music belongs to human universals, *i.e.* elements, patterns, features, or notions that are common to all human cultures worldwide, however, according to some opinions, it does not convey any biologically-relevant information. According to the mathematician and musicologist Guerino Mazzola "*music embodies meaningful communication and mediates physically between its emotional and symbolic layers.*"[4] The importance of music is exemplified by the discovery of Paleolithic musical instruments. Whereas most probably music at early times had no direct effect on the economy or a reproductive success, it may have had provided medium of social integration (Fig. 1). As of today, the influence of *muzak* on our decisions in supermarkets and retail centres proves its impact on real profits from these businesses. Nowadays music is one of the most ubiquitous human activity, independently on any social and cultural attributes or intellectual abilities.

Fig. 2. Prominent musical personalities : Sayed Darwish, Jim Morrison and Frederic Chopin portrayed on postage stamps of United Arab Republic, Germany and Soviet Union.

Fig. 3. Important political changes depicted on postage stamps : socialistic revolution in Bavaria (1918), Upper Silesia plebiscite (1921), Jordanian annexation of the West Bank (1948), the fall of the Nazi Germany (1945), formation of the Soviet Occupation Zone (1948), and the independence of Ukraine (1991).

The importance of music in modern society is unquestionable – composers, performers and musical instruments are leading motifs of numerous postage stamps (Fig. 2), along with monarchs, dictators, religion, nature and sport. Interestingly, in the past postage stamps (first introduced in 1840 by the United Kingdom) were considered as a very effective medium of communication. Therefore, each political or territorial change was (and still is) immediately reflected in postage stamps (Fig. 3). Year 1985 was announced European Year of Music (this fact was commemorated by a numerous series of stamps issued by European countries), and 2019 was announced the Smithsonian Year of Music.

Fig. 5. Tjlempung, totobuang, gangsa and kalintang: traditional musical instruments used in gamelan music.

Fig. 4. Examples of musical scores: Die Meistersinger von Nürnberg (R. Wagner) and 2nd Brandenburg Concerto (J.S. Bach) as depicted on German postage stamps.

Music and language are created and processed in distinctly different neural structures but have some common features: they are specific forms of communication, they have specific syntax and vocabulary – *i.e.* they have a set of elements (words or notes) and a set of rules (grammar or harmony and counterpoint) that govern the appropriate combination of these elements. Some kinds of music, like European tonal music, have strict syntax, some others (like dodecaphonic music) may be strictly

organized while at the same time lacking of audible regularities. Finally, there also exist genres, avant-garde, experimental music, and anti-music movements, which aim at breaking traditional regularities. Such exceptions and declared negation of musical syntax also confirms the existence of one. Music is a domain of human artistic and entertaining activity, but also a field of vigorous studies. Information alike, music is a very difficult notion to define in precise terms; dislike speech, it is not meant for direct communication purposes, especially of biological importance.[5] Conversely, it is meant to trigger various emotional responses in recipients due to aesthetical feelings. On the other hand, music is a very well-organized structure. Even the denial of the existence of such structure, conceptually declared by the author, proves the existence of specific "musical language" with appropriate grammar, syntax and vocabulary – the harmony, rhythmical patterns, timbres and their mutual relations. Therefore, not every combination of sounds should be considered as music. This indicates that music (like hardcore pornography) may be considered as a kind of an emotional communication of the « *I know it when I see it* » type.[6] Despite that, specific fractal signatures derived from compositions can be assigned to

Fig. 6. Sultan's tughra on old Saudi (1934) and Ottoman (1898) postage stamps.

Fig. 7. Circulation of goods and information as a decorative motif of postage stamps of Germany and Greece.

specific genres. The simplest musical message, melody, can be defined as an appropriate time sequence of quantized frequencies, usually noted as a musical score (Fig. 4).

These frequencies, called steps, are strictly defined by tuning systems. Most of musical systems are founded on a concept of the octave: an interval between frequencies of f and $2f$. Octave is an interval between the first and second harmonics of the harmonic series. Therefore, octave is considered as a natural phenomenon that has been referred to as the "*basic miracle of music*", the use of which is "*common in most musical systems.*"[7] There exist many different tuning systems,[8] and octave divisions (like Balinese and Javanese *gamelan* systems, Fig. 5). Other musical systems, both traditional (*e.g.* the Middle East, India and Far East), as well as modern experimental musical genres, use different intervals, including division of octave into 4, 5, 7, 34 (to name only a few possibilities), or even 96 equal steps, leading to the whole musical tuning continuum.[9]

These very strict structural rules and mathematical relations are naturally embedded in musical structures.[10] Current progress in computer

sciences, machine learning and artificial neural networks significantly influences musical creativity.[11] Unconventional computing is a natural consequence of research towards new computational paradigms and application of new materials and systems as computational platforms.[12] Therefore, some time ago, the composer Eduardo Miranda has initiated the multidisciplinary research and creative activity in the field at the border of music and unconventional computing.[13] Among the newest computational paradigms, *reservoir computing* is one of the latest discoveries.

Reservoir computing is a computational paradigm that explores the internal dynamics of physical systems for information processing. In principle, any physical system with internal dynamics can serve as a foundation for reservoir computing.[14] Dynamics at the edge of chaos renders a perfect medium for computation as it is the most sensitive for any perturbation of external signals (input data). Graphical representation of such dynamic behaviour usually resembles *tughra*, a calligraphic signature of a sultan, frequently found on postage stamps of Ottoman Empire and Saudi Arabia (Fig. 6).

Reservoirs must be also equipped with input and output ports. Any physical stimulus altering the internal dynamics can be considered as a carrier of information. The output in turn monitors the internal state of a part of the reservoir and is the only trainable (in the sense of machine learning) element of the whole device. Whereas the construction of a reservoir computer following the description given

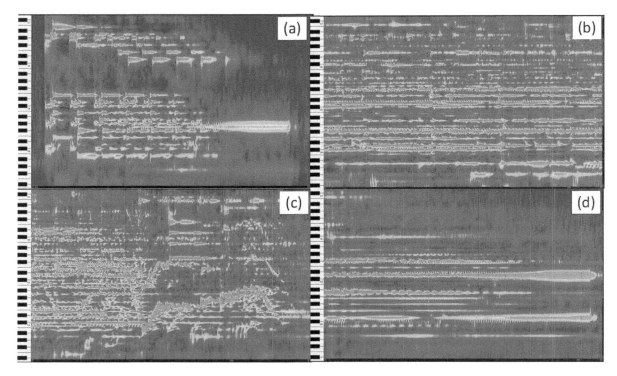

Fig. 8. Spectrograms calculated from the audio path of the Resevoir Study No. 1 world premiere recording.

above may pose significant difficulties, a simplified scheme based on a single nonlinear node equipped with a delayed feedback loop may be equally efficient from computational point of view, however much easier to build and operate. In such systems, the input signal (stream of data) circulates in a feedback loop and undergoes gradual changes (Fig. 7). The evolution of this signal serves as the reservoir state and is used for the generation of the output. This computational scheme has inspired us to compose and perform a piece of music inspired by the concept of reservoir computer.

The *Reservoir Study No. 1* (Marcin Strzelecki, 2019) scored for two electric guitars, cello, piano four hands and electronics is a composition in repetitive minimalism style. It is based on 555 ms delay feedback loop, which repeats and transforms music being played by a consort of musicians. These repetitions and transformations result in harmonic and timbral fluctuations of particular aesthetic quality. Numerous repetitions (both in the score and also added by the feedback) reflect dynamic changes inside the reservoir computer.

The Reservoir Study opens with a short improvisation of keyboard (Fig. 8a), that can be understood as an input for computation. These improvisations are followed by a slowly evolving tune, each bar is repeated four times and subsequently bars introduce subtle harmonic and timbral changes, as a very suggestive illustration of a revolution of signal in a feedback loop (Fig. 8b). In the middle part, this regular pace is suddenly broken and followed by another improvisation loaded with glissandi and irregular rhythmic patterns. Then the reservoir has reached the chaotic state (Fig. 8c)! Musical chaos slowly calms down and the regular pattern is reborn – the reservoir has reached the final state, which is the end of computation (Fig. 8d). Final chords represent the output layer generating the result of computation. World premiere performance of this piece was given by The Nano Consort (Konrad Szaciłowski – cello, Dawid Przyczyna, Kacper Pilarczyk – guitars, Marcin Strzelecki – keyboard, Dominika Peszko, Piotr Zieliński – piano) in Krakow Opera House, September 16th, 2019. Original recording is available as a supplementary material to our recent paper.[15]

This example illustrates the close relationship of contemporary music with unconventional computing, especially with the novel computational paradigms. It also shows how areas seemingly unrelated to art can become an inspiration for it and can be better understood thanks to it.

[1] PhD student (physics), guitarist, darbuka player, AGH University of Science and Technology, Kraków, Poland.

[2] Music theorist and composer, instrumentalist, Academy of Music in Kraków, Poland.

[3] Professor of chemistry, philatelist, AGH University of Science and Technology, Kraków, Poland.

[4] G. Mazzola, M. Mannone, Y. Pang, M. O'Brien, N. Torunski, *All about music. The complete Ontology: Realities, Semiotics, Communication and Embodiment*, Cham, Springer Nature, 2016.

[5] J. G. Roederer, *The physics and psychophysics of music*, New York, Springer Science+Business, 2008.

[6] P. Gewirtz, "On 'I Know It When I See It'," *Yale Law Journal 105*, 1996 1023-1047; "Jacobellis vs State of Ohio," *United States Supreme Court 378*, 1964, 184, available at https://openjurist.org/378/us/184.

[7] P. Cooper, *Perspectives in Music Theory: An Historical-Analytical Approach*, New York, Dodd, Mead and Co., 1973.

[8] R. Chuckrow, *Historical Tuning: Theory and Practice*, Briarcliff Manor, Rising Mist Publications, 2006.

[9] A. Milne, W. Sethares, J. Plamondon, "Dynamic Tonality: Extending the framework of tonality into the 21st Century," *Computer Music Journal 31*, 2007, 15-32; E. Blackwood, *The Structure of Recognizable Diatonic Tunings*, Princeton, Princeton University Press, 1985.

[10] G. Loy, *Musimatics*, Cambridge, MIT Press, 2006; L. M. Zbikowski, *Foundations of musical grammar*, Oxford, Oxford University Press, 2017.

[11] G. Nierhaus, *Algorithmic composition. Paragidms of automated music generation*, Wien, Springer, 2009; R. T. Dean, A. McLean, *The Oxford Handbook of Algorithmic Music*, Oxford, Oxford University Press, 2018.

[12] A. Adamatzky (ed.), *Advances in Unconventional Computing Theory*, Springer International Publishing, 2017; A. Adamatzky (ed.), *Advances in Unconventional Computing. Prototypes, Models and Algorithms*, Springer International Publishing, 2017; A. Adamatzky, S. G. Akl, G. C. Sirakoulis, From Parallel to Emergent Computing, Boca Raton, CRC Press, 2019.

[13] E. R. Miranda (ed.), *Guide to unconventional computing for music*, Cham, Springer Nature, 2017.

[14] V. Athanasiou, Z. Konkoli, "On mathematics of universal computation with generic dynamical systems," in A. Adamatzky, S.G. Akl, G.C. Sirakoulis (eds.), *From Parallel to emergent computing*, CRC Press, London, 2019.

[15] D. Przyczyna, P. Zawal, T. Mazur, M. Strzelecki, P.L. Gentili, K. Szaciłowski, "In-materio neuromimetic devices: dynamics, information processing and pattern recognition," *Japanese Journal of Applied Physics 59(5)*, 2020, 050504.

Unconventional sensing: doing it unusual way in unusual settings

Zoran Konkoli[1]

The standard way of sensing implies a linear flow of information, from the object we wish to analyse towards the observer. The object of interest will be referred to as "the environment." The environment can be many things, a temperature in a room or the amount of cracks in the material. The usual sensor is like a factory line where the flow of information is well understood and every step is carefully engineered. Normally, a sensing instance is a one-time event. It can be, and often is, repeated, leaving the impression of continuity. We know exactly how every part of the sensor is supposed to behave. But it is a one-time event nevertheless and the execution of every sensing event is always nearly the same. But there are other ways of doing sensing, and over the course of the last few years we have explored a novel, somewhat unconventional way of sensing, to be referred to as the SWEET sensing approach. SWEET is more a template than it is an approach. The SWEET is an algorithmic template for building intelligent sensing substrates. The user is supposed to engineer different instances of it depending on the situation. The typical SWEET sensing process is very flexible, and is essentially a dynamic process, where the single time instance is irrelevant, but rather the behaviour over an extended time interval is of paramount importance. It is a sort of indirect sensing which happens through a proxy. There is an ongoing dialogue between the observer and the proxy, in which the observer accumulates small clues proxy provides about the system of interest. In turns, the proxy also accumulates information through a dialogue. This article summarizes how such an unconventional sensing setup can be realized and what its essential ingredients are. The main objective is to present the material in a pedagogical way so that colleagues from other disciplines can understand the method and use it to solve their problems.

The standard way of sensing implies a linear flow of information, from the object we wish to analyse, the environment, towards the observer. In sensing applications the "environment" can be many things, a temperature in the room, the amount of cracks in the material, or the amount of rare molecules in a unit volume of solvent. The usual sensor works according to well-understood principles which are carefully engineered. There are no surprises. The flow of information is linear. Further, a traditional sensing instance is a one-time event. Events like these are often repeated in time, which might give an impression of continuous sensing, even some sort of intelligence perhaps, but in reality such sensing events are discrete separate events. To gain a time perspective on the observed data, one needs to engineer an external intelligence that can gather information obtained from the sensor, and further process it. The typical time to execute the sensing event is much smaller than the times that separate these events. Sensing instances can occur at an equally spaced intervals, or when triggered by a control mechanism. Regardless of the engineering details, we are talking about a one-time event since the execution of the sensing event is always nearly the same, and we know exactly how every part of the sensor is supposed to behave. In fact failing to do so is considered to be a malfunction. The typical sensing setup is show in the figure below. However, there are other ways of doing sensing.

Over the course of the last few years we have explored a novel, somewhat unconventional way of sensing where irregularity and temporal aspects of the sensor's dynamics are of

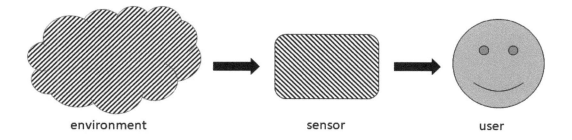

Fig. 1. The traditional sensing setup. The flow of information is linear.

paramount importance, the SWEET sensing setup.[2] The SWEET sensing setup is an algorithmic template. The most important components are depicted in the figure below. Though the SWEET sensing setup has been developed with a particular application in mind, the analysis of time series data, it is very likely that the setup could be used to solve problems featuring in other disciplines, but more on that later. The details will of course differ depending on the implementation context. Our own work[3] covered some problems related to ionic sensing with ion sensitive electronic components, such as an organic transistor and a memristor. The SWEET sensing process is very flexible, and is essentially a dynamic process, where the single time instance is irrelevant, but rather the behaviour over an extended time interval is of paramount importance. It is a sort of indirect sensing which happens through proxy and it happens in a dialogue form. A similar indirect sensing idea has been suggested in 2006[4] but, surprisingly, has not been pursued rigorously. The authors have shown that by monitoring the changes in the structure of the feedback apparatus that controls the robot it is possible to infer about the environment that the robot resides in.

The SWEET approach is an algorithmic template for realizing the indirect sensing idea in the context of time-series data analysis where the notion of time and remembering history is treated as an opportunity rather than a problem. The notion of time is extremely important as there is an ongoing dialogue between the environment and the proxy. The proxy (sensing reservoir)[5] is an environment sensitive dynamical system. It is affected by the environment, but the details of the proxy interacts with the environment are not important from an engineering point of view. It might appear that this interaction is a one-way information channel where the information propagates from the environment into the proxy. To some extent this is true, as the proxy is not supposed to influence the environment. However, the proxy updates its state recurrently, where the state of the proxy at a particular time instance depends on its previous state and the information it has received from the environment.

Through the dialogue with an environment (cf. fig. 2, dialogue 1) the proxy is pushed towards a certain state, and the state of the proxy encodes all previous instances of environment-proxy interaction. Perhaps, one could think of it as a one-way dialogue, in the same way as a psychotherapist gets to know his patient. Through this dialogue, the proxy accumulates small clues about the environment of interest, which a traditional setup might simply miss. Again, it is important to realize that this would be impossible without a memory of the past, the system used as a proxy would "forget" every bit of information it has collected.

There is a second dialogue going on, the one between the observer and the proxy (indicated by dialogue 2 in fig. 2). This second dialogue happens through two mechanisms: (a) the fixed instructions in the form of a drive signal, and (b) through a feedback. In many instances, this feedback can greatly improve the performance of a device. The feedback mechanism

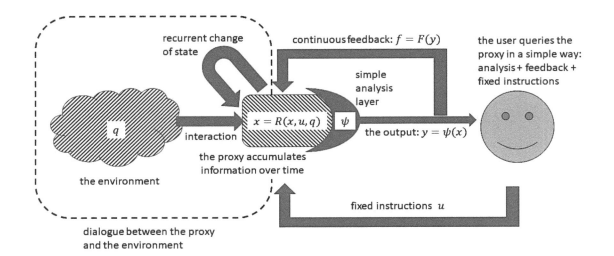

Fig. 2. The SWEET sensing setup. Dialogue 1: There is an ongoing dialogue between the environment and the proxy. During this dialogue the proxy accumulates the information about the environment. Dialogue 2: The user interacts with the proxy in a simple way to infer what the environment looks like.

has the tendency to make the system "sharper" or simply more "intelligent," especially if it is provided with a delay in time. This improvement is a well-known fact,[6] and is nothing specificity to the SWEET setup. The delay can be explicitly engineered, but it can be also an intrinsic part of a dynamical system since such systems clearly exhibit some sort of "memory behaviour". The state of a dynamical system depends on everything that the system experienced in the past. Furthermore, dynamical systems might have the ability to "propagate" behaviour through the system to different locations, which could bounce around, causing a natural delay. All very exciting possibilities. Perhaps the simplest way of explaining the SWEET sensing concept is through the following thought experiment (*cf.* fig. 3):

- *The sensing problem (the environment):* Imagine that we are sitting in a room without windows and that we are interested in the weather outside. Thus the object of our interest is the weather. However, we are not allowed to open the window and peek out to see what the weather is like. Likewise, we are not allowed to use the phone or any other means of communication with the external world.

- *The proxy:* A person comes into the room and we are allowed to interact with the person to figure out what the weather is like. This is our only chance to infer about the weather.

- *The interaction with the proxy:* By assumptions, we are not allowed to ask direct questions like "What is the weather like outside?" This constraint is very common in practical applications that are close to engineering. We cannot interact with the proxy in any way we please. There are likely going to be constraints imposed on how we can interact with any system. For example, we cannot easily measure the positions of all atoms in a gas. We could try to measure their average velocity, which gives us an idea about the temperature of the gas. Thus to illustrate that aspect of the problem, in our thought experiment we are restricting the way we can interact with our human proxy. Naturally, the more direct questions one can ask the better. However, the main idea is to "interview" the person about the weather. Ask small questions and try to assess what they imply. Here the emphasis is on the full set of answers we are getting, not on a particular answer to a specific question. The way we can interact with the proxy is critical. For example, if we can assume that we can observe the person, we could try to see if the person carries a wet umbrella. A wet umbrella would imply that very likely there is a rain outside. But one cannot be sure. It could have rained few hours earlier but we cannot be certain. Even a dry umbrella might imply a bad weather. For example, it could be that it is cloudy outside. Clearly, if we are not allowed to ask a direct question, the dialogue is the best option. Through a dialogue we can acquire information. For example, we can ask the person how she/he feels like. If the person appears grumpy, then it might have to do with the bad weather, but there could be other reasons. For example the person might have lost a shoe, and that could be inferred from follow up questions. If the person appears happy, very likely the weather is nice. But, again, we cannot be sure. The person could have won the lottery, and more

follow up questions would be needed to determine this.

- *The feedback mechanism:* In this particular instance a useful feedback mechanism would be to ask some provocative questions. For example, if the person is happy, we might try to provoke the person into angry response and from that judge the original "degree of happiness" that the person had before he/she entered the room. Likewise, if the person appears calm, we could ask provocative questions to see if there is some discontent lurking behind the surface. All this would indicate that we are likely dealing with the case of the bad weather.

In fact, the sensing solutions we envision resemble a thought experiment discussed above. The SWEET setup mimics the way of how humans communicate experiences and process exchanged information, rather than how a machine would perform similar tasks. This article explores the ways of realizing the human

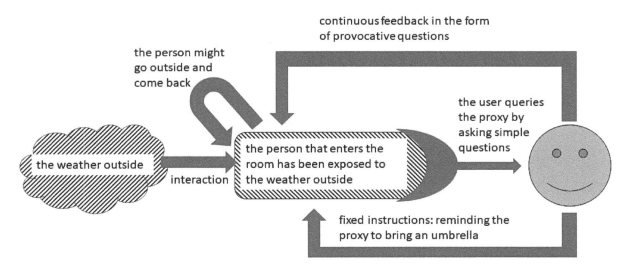

Fig. 3. An example of implementing the SWEET sensing setup.

way of understanding and analysing environment in the engineering context. This is the main point behind the SWEET sensing setup. Instead of a human one uses a generic dynamical system as a proxy. In pretty much the same way as the mental state of mind of a human is influenced by weather, so is the state of the dynamical system influenced by the environment. The existence of this interaction is the minimal requirement for the SWEET setup to work. However, the trademark of our sensing setup is that it is extremely flexible.

Why should one bother with such unconventional sensing setups? There are several reasons, ranging from pure engineering/practical towards more profound:

To begin with, there are many instances in the information processing engineering where the goal is to collect and analyze information *in situ*. For example, in the traditional setup, remote sensors might collect information and channel it to a huge data center where this information is *stored* and *processed*. However, the disadvantage with such a setup is that one might need to both store large amounts of data, and most importantly, perhaps, arrive at simple conclusions, after all the fuss. It is much better to make such conclusions locally, and simply send the results of the analysis. For example, a bridge operator only needs to know one bit of information, whether the bridge is stable or about to collapse or in somewhat simplified language "everything under control" versus "trouble." It is much simpler to send this information instead of constantly streaming sensor data from dozens of sensors.

The more subtle reason is as follows. The whole SWEET setup is powered by a very simple idea discussed above, and because of that it is extremely flexible. Since SWEET is a template, an engineer only needs to implement its key mathematical abstractions (essentially the various forms of the dialogues introduced earlier). Of course, this is a bit of oversimplification (if it were that easy), but in the nutshell this is what needs to happen. Regardless of the practical difficulties the implementation strategy is very clear. One can think of the SWEET setup as a very generic user manual, where the user can exercise a great deal of flexibility in

implementing. One might think of it as a "religious text" in which the principles are given but the followers are supposed to interpret it and apply it in everyday life. Because of that, our sensing ideas could be of relevance for other areas of human endeavour, including humanistic sciences.

Naturally, one might even have to modify the setup depending on the problem but the core idea of a two-fold dialogue will likely survive if the setup is applied in other areas:

> We have investigated numerous options ourselves. All the sensing problems we have investigated hatched from vastly different application contexts: monitoring ionic solution for rare ions that are hard to detect, monitoring ECG (electrocardiogram) signals using simple hardware, predicting chance for the occurrence of sepsis for intensive care patients. These might be considered as standard engineering problems, very typical for natural sciences.
>
> We gave a serious thought of applying the SWEET sensing setup to tackle a range of completely unrelated problems to the ones we published on. We have thought about other much more "crazy" ideas such as helping spine-cord injuries to heal, we have explored some innovative information processing options in the IoT (Internet of Things) context related to creating a gigantic intelligent sensing substrate to realize distributed sensing, and believe it or not envisioned the setup to enhance human learning, and finally tried to think about ways of enhancing the outcome of a psychotherapy session.

These rather bold aspirations listed above ought to justify the title.

[1] Professor at Chalmers University of Technology, Goteborg, Sweden.

[2] Z. KONKOLI, "On developing theory of reservoir computing for sensing applications: the state weaving environment echo tracker (SWEET) algorithm," *International Journal of Parallel, Emergent and Distributed Systems*, 2016, 121-143.

[3] V. ATHANASIOU *et al.*, "On Sensing Principles Using Temporally Extended Bar Codes," *IEEE Sensors Journal*

20(13), 2020, 6782-6791; V. Athanasiou & Z. Konkoli, "On Improving The Computing Capacity of Dynamical Systems," Scientific Reports 10(1), 2020, 9191; V. Athanasiou & Z. Konkoli, "Memristor Models for Early Detection of Sepsis in ICU Patients," *Computing in Cardiology (CinC)*, 2019; Z. Konkoli et al., "Reservoir computing with computational matter," in M. Amos, S. Rasmussen, and S. Stepney (eds.), *Computational Matter*, Cham, Springer, 2018; V. Athanasiou & Z. Konkoli, "On using reservoir computing for sensing applications: exploring environment-sensitive memristor networks," *International Journal of Parallel, Emergent and Distributed Systems*, 2017.

[4] F. Iida & R. Pfeifer, "Sensing through body dynamics," *Robotics and Autonomous Systems 54(8)*, 2006, 631-640.

[5] Z. Konkoli, "On developing theory of reservoir computing for sensing applications: the state weaving environment echo tracker (SWEET) algorithm," *op. cit.*

[6] L. Appeltant et al., "Information processing using a single dynamical node as complex system," *Nature Communications 2*, 2011, 468/1-6. See Vasseleu's poignant discussion of "fantasies of disembodied mastery" in C. Vasseleu, "Virtual Bodies/Virtual Worlds," *Australian Feminist Studies 19*, 1994, 155-169. For a critical discussion of "contemporary technoscientific corporealizations of the 'almost human,'" see C. Castaneda, L. Suchman, "Robot visions," *Social Studies of Science 44(3)*, 2014, 315-341.

Induction versus Deduction in Science, Computing, Literature and Art

Mark Burgin[1]

Induction and deduction are important cognitive processes, which exist in all spheres of human culture. These processes are analyzed, formalized and utilized in logic and mathematics. However, to better understand their essence, we examine these processes using theoretical tools of computer science and describing their role in science, computing, literature and art.

As a cognitive mechanism, *deduction* is a type of logical inference of knowledge performed by application of specific deduction rules having, in general, the form

$$A \rightarrow B$$

or

$$A \vdash B$$

where *A* is called the *assumption* of the rule, *B* is called the *conclusion* of the rule, and both of them consist of a finite number of expressions, formulas or statements.

For instance, taking the expression "*X* is equal to *Y*" with variables *X* and *Y*, we can build the formal deduction rule

"*U* is equal to *V*"& "*V* is equal to *W*" ⊢ "*U* is equal to *W*"

It means

If *U* is equal to *V* and *V* is equal to *W*, then *U* is equal to *W*.

Recursive algorithms and the majority of logical systems formalize deduction, which became the basic inference tool in logic and mathematics.[2] In mathematics, the term *deduction* is often used as a synonym of the term *proof*.

At the same time, mathematical and scientific practice shows that deduction is used not so much for knowledge production as for knowledge justification because, as Aristotle observed, scientific discovery by deduction is impossible, except one knows the "first" primary premises, and it is necessary to obtain these premises by induction.[3]

As a cognitive mechanism, *induction* is a form of logical inference that allows inferring a general statement from a sufficient number of particular cases, which provide *evidence* for the general statement induced (the conclusion). However, if the evidence is not complete, the conclusion may be incorrect. For instance, Aristotle saw that all of the swans in the places he lived were white, so he induced that all swans are white in general. However, much later, Europeans came to Australia and discovered black swans. This shows that in contrast to deduction, induction does not always give correct results because it works with incomplete information, while the number of initial cases usually is not bounded and the researcher does not know for sure when to stop. However, the whole science is actually built on induction because scientific laws have to be in agreement with nature for natural sciences and with social systems for social sciences, while it is possible to make only a finite number of experiments.

Naturally, there is also inductive learning, which involves making uncertain inferences that go beyond direct experience and are based on intuition and insight.

However, this is only one kind of induction – *empirical induction*, correct application of which demands highly developed intuition and can be invalidated by some new observations or experiments. There is also *mathematical induction*.

Mathematicians, being largely dissatisfied by absence of absolute reliability in empirical induction used by physicists and other scientists, elaborated mathematical induction, which, in essence, reduces induction to deduction by the *axiom of induction*, which is very popular in mathematics and has several forms.

While mathematical induction eliminates necessity of intuition in making the conclusion, acceptance of the axiom of induction and its application still demand intuition.[4]

Interestingly, the progress in computer science and mathematics was achieved by going from the models of computation based on deduction, such as *Turing machines*, to the models of computation based on empirical (scientific) induction, such as *inductive Turing machines*.

Let us consider these models.

In his pioneering paper published in 1936, Turing clearly explains that his a-machine, later called Turing machine, mathematically models the work of a human computer. We can also add that it models the work of an accountant. In both cases, the goal of the process is computation of values of functions according to exact (mechanical) rules and stopping when the result is obtained.

> "The idea behind digital computers may be explained by saying that these machines are intended to carry out any operations which could be done by a human computer. The human computer is supposed to be following fixed rules; he has no authority to deviate from them in any detail. We may suppose that these rules are supplied in a book, which is altered whenever he is put on to a new job. He has also an unlimited supply of paper on which he does his calculations. He may also do his multiplications and additions on a 'desk machine', but this is not important."[5]

The work of a scientist or mathematician is essentially different because in essence, it is exploration, which can include calculation but cannot be reduced to it. This situation is reflected in the status of scientific theories and laws in general and the theories and laws of physics, in particular. For instance, Stephen Hawking writes:

> "Any physical theory is always provisional, in the sense that it is only a hypothesis: you can never prove it. No matter how many times the results of experiments agree with some theory, you can never be sure that the next time the result will not contradict the theory."[6]

That is why, in science, *e.g.*, in physics or biology, we can observe the following process of research.

First, scientist learn something about results of other scientists in their area.

Second (this step is sometimes skipped), scientists conduct some experiments and collect experimental data.

Third, scientists elaborate a hypothesis *L* often formulating it in mathematical terms.

Fourth, scientists conduct new experiments and check the hypothesis *L*.

Fifth, if a sufficient number of experiments support their hypothesis, scientists call *L* a law of nature.

Note that experiments are not only physical but also mental. Mental experiments are especially popular in mathematics.

As the time goes, the following situations are possible.

> (a) Whenever all further experiments related to the law *L* support *L*, this law *L* is accepted forever as a law of nature.
>
> (b) A new experiment contradicts *L*. In this case, either it is declared that *L* is not a law of nature or it is assumed that *L* is not valid in the initial domain. In both cases, *L* is rejected as a law of nature (either completely or for the initial domain) and scientists start searching for the new law, which more correctly than *L* describes the experimental data.

We can see that this process exactly reflects how an inductive Turing machine is functioning.[7] Note that if inductive Turing machines obtain their results, they do this in finite time, *i.e.*, making only a finite number of steps. They mathematically describe and formalize empirical induction, that is, inductive reasoning prevalent in science and mathematics. Note that induction used in science is not mathematical induction, which reduces induction to deduction.

Thus, we come to the following conclusion:

Turing machine formalizes the work of an accountant or a human computer.
Inductive Turing machine formalizes the work of a scientist and functioning of science.

Creative work of scientists, which includes scientific induction, belongs to a higher level in the hierarchy of intellectual activity in comparison with the reproductive work of accountants.[8]

Hence, it is natural that inductive Turing machines can do much more than Turing machines and this feature of inductive Turing machines is mathematically proved.[9] In particular, inductive Turing machines can solve problems that cannot be solved by any Turing machine.

As a supportive evidence (not a proof) for the above statement, it is possible to take what Kurt Gödel wrote in a note entitled "A philosophical error in Turing's work":

> "Turing gives an argument which is supposed to show that mental procedures cannot go beyond mechanical procedures. However, this argument is inconclusive. What Turing disregards completely is the fact that mind, in its use, is not static, but constantly developing, i.e., we understand abstract terms more and more precisely as we go on using them... though at each stage the number and precision of the abstract terms at our disposal may be finite, both... may converge toward infinity..."[10]

Implementing both empirical induction and deduction, inductive Turing machines provide more efficient tools for artificial intelligence (AI) in comparison with Turing machines or other recursive algorithms.[11] This is important because researchers explain that recursive algorithms are not adequate tools for AI.[12] Indeed, inductive Turing machines are much more powerful than Turing machines.[13] While Turing machines generate only two lowest levels of the infinite arithmetical hierarchy used as measurement tool of the power of automata and computing machines, inductive Turing machines of higher orders can generate the whole arithmetical hierarchy.[14] Invention of inductive Turing machines changed the concept of algorithm essentially extending its scope and power.[15] It was a transformation of the computing paradigm in the sense of Kuhn,[16] symbolizing emergence and proliferation of a new type of algorithms called super-recursive algorithms.

Later, other classes of abstract automata that also perform inductive computations – inductive cellular automata,[17] inductive evolutionary machines[18] and periodic Turing machines[19] – were constructed.

In addition to the individual level of a scientist, induction is prevalent in science as a whole. It is possible to find a methodological analysis of inductive processes in Kuhn's and Prigogine & Stengers' works.[20]

However, inductive processes are not bounded by the domain of science – they exist in many other areas, including art and literature. For instance, writing about discourse, Paul Ricoeur stresses that there is always a surplus of meaning that goes beyond what objective techniques seek to explain.[21] There is a surplus of meaning because we apply objective techniques to things we already understand as having a possible meaning without fully exhausting that meaning. The meaning of acts of discourse is moreover always open to new interpretations, particularly as time passes and the very context in which interpretation takes place changes. Consequently, we once more come to inductive processes.

The same is true for the true creations of art and literature. For instance, Leonardo da Vinci wrote "Art is never finished, only abandoned." In a similar vein, Pablo Picasso asserted:

> "To finish a work? To finish a picture? What nonsense! To finish it means to be through with it, to kill it, to rid it of its soul, to give it its final blow the coup de grace for the painter as well as for the picture."

This naturally implies that, at least, for some artists the process of creation follows inductive footsteps.

Besides, comprehension and understanding of artistic creations is a kind of discourse and creations of art and literature, especially profound ones, are always open to new interpretations. Culture is changing. Knowledge of people is changing. It brings necessity in new and new interpretations and commentaries. Consequently, we once more come to inductive processes.

In addition, natural languages and especially languages of art convey more than a single meaning. Thus, text in these languages can always be understood in more than one way.

Hence, texts regularly need to be interpreted and reinterpreted while interpretation is an inductive process by its very nature.

As it was already exhibited, even creation of insightful works in art and literature involves inductive processes. For instance, La Rochefoucauld had difficulties arranging his maxims. He issued no fewer than five editions in his lifetime, all with significant alterations, deletions, and addenda. In the fifth edition of 1678, his publisher apologetically notes, *"As for the order of these reflections, you will easily appreciate that it was difficult to arrange them in any order, because all of them deal with different subjects."*[22]

Even more explicitly this trait was expressed when in his conversations with the Russian Music Professor Aleksandr Borisovich Goldenveizer, Leo Tolstoy characterized the creative work of an artist saying:

> *"I can't understand how anyone can write without rewriting everything over and over again. I scarcely ever re-read my published writings, but if by chance I come across a page, it always strikes me: All this must be rewritten; this is how I should have written it."*

This distinctly demonstrates that for Tolstoy writing was an inductive process.

Thus, we can see that inductive processes pervade in all kinds of creative human activities while mathematically they are modeled by inductive Turing machines.

[1] UCLA, Los Angeles, CA 90095, USA.
[2] M. Burgin, *Super-recursive Algorithms*, New York, Springer, 2005; D. Deutch, *The beginning of infinity*, London, Penguin Books Ltd, 2011.
[3] Aristotle, *The Complete Work of Aristotle*, ed. J. Barnes, Princeton, Princeton University Press, 1984.
[4] H. Poincaré, *La valeur de la science*, Paris, Flammarion, 1905.
[5] A. Turing, "On Computable Numbers with an Application to the Entscheidungs-problem," *Proc. Lond. Math. Soc. Ser.2 42*, 1936, 230-265.
[6] S. W. Hawking, *A Brief History of Time*, Toronto/New York/London, Bantam Books, 1988.
[7] M. Burgin, "Nonlinear Phenomena in Spaces of Algorithms," *International Journal of Computer Mathematics 80(12)*, 2003, 1449-1476.

[8] M. Burgin, "Intellectual activity in creative work," in *Forms of knowledge representation and creative thinking*, Novosibirsk, 1989, 53-56 (in Russian).
[9] M. Burgin, "Nonlinear Phenomena in Spaces of Algorithms," *op. cit.*; M. Burgin, *Super-recursive Algorithms, op. cit.*
[10] K. Gödel, *Collected Works, Vol. II, Publications 1938-1974*, Oxford, Oxford University Press, 1990.
[11] M. Burgin, "On the power of oracles in the context of hierarchical intelligence," *Journal of Artificial Intelligence Research & Advances 3(2)*, 2016, 6-17; M. Burgin, "Inductive Turing Machines," in A. Adamatzky (ed.), *Unconventional Computing, A volume in the Encyclopedia of Complexity and Systems Science*, Berlin/Heidelberg, Springer, 2018, 675-688.
[12] A. Sloman, "The Irrelevance of Turing machines to AI," in M. Scheutz (ed.), *Computationalism: New Directions*, Cambridge, MIT Press, 2002, 87-127 (http://www.cs.bham.ac.uk/~axs/).
[13] M. Burgin, *Super-recursive Algorithms, op. cit.*
[14] M. Burgin, "Nonlinear Phenomena in Spaces of Algorithms," *op. cit.*
[15] M. Burgin, "The Notion of Algorithm and the Church-Turing Thesis," *VIII International Congress on logic, methodology and philosophy of science*, Moscow, 1987, v. 5, pt. 1, 138-140; M. Burgin, "How We Know What Technology Can Do," *Communications of the ACM 44(11)*, 2001, 82-88.
[16] T. S. Kuhn, *The Structure of Scientific Revolutions*, Chicago, University of Chicago Press, 1962.
[17] M. Burgin, "Inductive Cellular Automata," *International Journal of Data Structures and Algorithms 1(1)*, 2015, 1-9.
[18] M. Burgin & E. Eberbach, "Evolutionary Automata: Expressiveness and Convergence of Evolutionary Computation," *Computer Journal 55(9)*, 2012, 1023-1029.
[19] M. Burgin, "Periodic Turing Machines," *Journal of Computer Technology & Applications (JoCTA) 5(3)*, 2014, 6-18.
[20] T. S. Kuhn, *The Structure of Scientific Revolutions, op. cit.*; I. Prigogine & I. Stengers, *Order out of Chaos*, Toronto/New York/London, Bantam Books, 1984.
[21] P. Ricoeur, *Hermeneutics and the Human Sciences: Essays on Language, Action and Interpretation*, ed. & trans. J. B. Thompson, Cambridge, Cambridge University Press, 1981.
[22] Cf. A. Hui, *A Theory of the Aphorism: From Confucius to Twitter*, Princeton/Oxford, Princeton University Press, 2019.

Fungal Grey Matter

Andrew Adamatzky[1] and Irina Petrova[2]

Fungi are creatures with remarkably pronounced protocognition abilities. They control 'thinking' of trees. They open minds of humans. They help us to live in the world and to see the invisible. Recently we discovered that the electrical activity of fungi is similar to neurons. Fungi communicate with trains of spikes of electrical potential. Fungi respond to stimulation by changing their electrical properties and patterns of their electrical activity. Here, we briefly overview our discoveries on sensing and computing with fungi.

Fig. 1. Irina Petrova, *Deep Down the Rabbit Hole*. Installation with *Macrolepiota procera* fungi, 2020.

Fungi are the first creatures which arrived on our planet. They are creatures of magic. They populate a thin layer of soil, just under the surface and implement chemical, and possibly electrical communication between trees and plants. There is a chance that when sending a message from one tree to another fungi do actually alter the meaning of the messages thus controlling 'thinking' of trees and ultimately governing a Mind of the Forest. To some degree fungi also shaped a Mind of Noosphere. From the beginning of civilisations fungi have been an essential component of the spiritual cere-monies, rituals, community building events, healing, mind opening inspirational trips and mental healings. No one will ever forget their first trip with Psilocybin mushrooms and will always be grateful to shrooms for showing un-seeable. Here we discuss how electro-physi-ological properties of fungi can be used in sensing and information, in unconventional computing.

A vibrant field of unconventional computing aims to employ space-time dynamics of phys-ical, chemical and biological media to design novel computational techniques, architectures and working prototypes of embedded comput-ing substrates and devices. Interaction-based computing devices is one of the most diverse and promising families of the unconventional computing structures.[3] They are based on in-teractions of fluid streams, signals propagating along conductors or excitation wave-fronts. Typically, logical gates and their cascade im-plemented in an excitable medium are 'hand-crafted' to address exact timing and type of interactions between colliding wave-fronts. The artificial design of logical circuits might be suitable when chemical media or function-al materials are used. However, the approach might be not feasible when embedding com-putation in living systems, where the architec-ture of conductive pathways may be difficult to alter or control. During the last decade we produced nearly forty prototypes of sensing and computing devices from the slime mould *Physarum polycephalum*, including shortest path finders, computational geometry proces-sors, hybrid electronic devices.[4] We found that the slime mould is a convenient substrate for unconventional computing however geometry of the slime mould's protoplasmic networks is continuously changing, thus preventing fab-rication of long-living devices, and the slime mould computing devices are confined to ex-perimental laboratory setups. Fungi *Basidio-mycetes* are now taxonomically distinct from the slime mould, however their development and behaviour are phenomenologically simi-lar: mycelium networks are analogous to the slime mould's protoplasmic networks, and the fruit bodies are analogous to the slime mould's

stalks of sporangia. *Basidiomycetes* are less susceptible to infections, when cultured in-doors, especially commercially available species, they are larger in size and more con-venient to manipulate than slime mould, and they could be easily found and experimented with outdoors. This makes the fungi an ideal object for developing future living computing devices. Availability and scalability of fungi is yet another advantage. The fungi is a largest, widely distributed and the oldest group of liv-ing organisms. Smallest fungi are microscopic single cells. The largest fungi, *Armillaria bulbo-sa*, occupies 15 hectares and weighs 10 tons, and the largest fruit body belongs to *Fomitipo-ria ellipsoidea* which at 20 years old is 11 m long, 80 cm wide, 5 cm thick and has estimat-ed weight of nearly half-a-ton.

Fig. 2. Fungi *P. ostreatus* explores space while geometrically constrained.

Spiking fungi

Not only neurons spike. Action potential-like spikes of electrical potential have been discovered using intracellular recording of mycelium of *Neurospora crassa*[5] and further confirmed in intra-cellular recordings of action potential in hypha of *Pleurotus ostreatus* and *Armillaria bulbosa*[6] and in extracellular recordings of fruit bodies and of substrates colonized by mycelium of *Pleurotus ostreatus*.[7] While the exact nature of the travelling spikes remains uncertain we can speculate, by drawing analogies with oscillations of electrical potential of slime mould,[8] that the spikes in fungi are triggered by calcium waves, reversing of cytoplasmic flow, translocation of nutrients and metabolites. Studies of electrical activity of higher plants can bring us even more clues.[9] Thus, the plants use the electrical spikes for a long-distance communication aimed to coordinate an activity of their bodies. The spikes of electrical potential in plants relate to a motor activity, responses to changes in temperature, osmotic environment and mechanical stimulation. In experiments with *Pleurotus ostreatus*[10] we demonstrated that fruit bodies of oyster fungi exhibit trains of action-like spike of extracellularly recorded electrical potential. We observed two types of spikes: high-frequency spikes, duration nearly 3~min, and low-frequency spikes, duration nearly 14~min. The spikes are observed in trains of 10-30 spikes. The depolarisation and repolarisation rates of both types of spikes are the same. Refractory period of a high-frequency spike is one sixth of the spike's period, and of a low-frequency spike one third of the spike's period. We showed that fruit bodies respond with spikes of electrical potential in response to physical, chemical and thermal stimulation; not only a simulated body responds with a spike but other fruit bodies of the cluster respond as well. We believe the spikes of electrical potential travelling in mycelium networks play the same roles of information carriers as action potential travelling along neural pathways in *e.g.* human brains. Thus it would be advantageous to discover what types of information processing devices we could make from fungi. To make information processing devices from fungi we can either use fungi as electronic components of analog computers or employ internal dynamics of excitation in fungi directly. Both options are illustrated below.

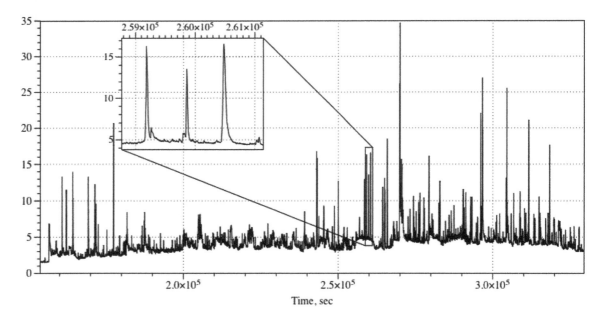

Fig. 3. Example of electrical spiking activity recorded from a hemp substrate colonised by mycelium of *P. ostreatus*.

48

Fungal electronics

Fungi are memristors. The memristor is a device whose resistance changes depending on the polarity and magnitude of a voltage applied to the device's terminals. A memristor is a material logical implication. Therefore any logical circuits can be made purely from the memristors. We have examined the conducted current for a given voltage applied as a function of the previous voltage to fungi fruiting bodies and substrates colonised by fungi, and showed that the fungi exhibit remarkable memristive properties.[11] Indeed, demonstrating that a fruit body or a substrate colonised by fungi exhibit memristive properties is a just tiny step forward: cascading fungal memristors into function circuits will be the challenging task.

mycelium can be used as part of a capacitors array. A fungal electronic circuit could have chemical, mechanical or optical inputs.

A range of fungal responses to stimulation have been discovered in our experiments[13] with fungal skin[14] – a thin flexible sheet of a living homogeneous mycelium made by a filamentous fungus. We demonstrated that a thin sheet of homogeneous living mycelium of *Ganoderma resinaceum* shows pronounced electrical responses to mechanical and optical stimulation. It is possible to differentiate between the fungal skin's response to mechanical and optical stimulation. The fungal skin responds to mechanical stimulation with a 15 min spike of electrical potential, which diminishes even if the applied pressure on the skin remains. The

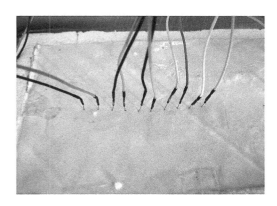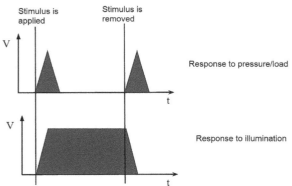

Fig. 4. Responsive fungal skin.
Left, pairs of differential electodes inserted in the fungal skin of *G. resinaceum*.
Right, response of the fungal skin to pressure and illumination.

Despite being logically universal, memristors might not be enough to build fully functional computing circuits. We might need to store energy, implement digital memory, do signal coupling and decoupling, make high-pass and low-pass filters, suppress noise. All these can be done with capacitors. Fungi are capacitors, albeit rapidly discharging. In laboratory experiments we showed that the capacitance of mycelium is in the order of hundreds of pico-Farads and the charge density of the mycelium decays rapidly with increasing distance from the source probes.[12] Nevertheless, the

skin responds to optical stimulation by raising its electrical potential and keeping it raised till the light is switched off. We can even differentiate the responses to loading and removal of the weight. Whilst amplitudes of 'loading' and 'removal' spikes are the same (0.4 mV in average) the fungal skin average reaction time to removal of the weight is 2.4 times shorter than the reaction to loading of the weight (385 sec versus 911 sec). Also 'loading' spikes are 1.6 times wider than 'removal' spikes (1261 sec versus 774 sec).

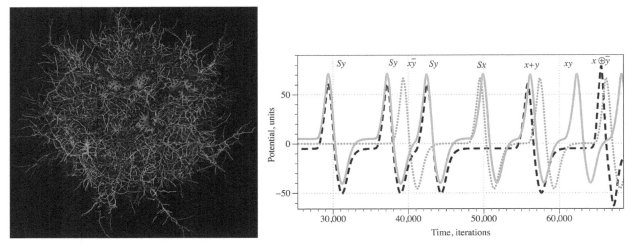

Fig. 5. Computing with travelling spikes in mycelium networks. Left, a snapshot of an excitation waves propagating in the network. Right, encoding of the spiking response to Boolean gates.

Fungal computing

Mycelium networks are disorganized and difficult to program at a fine-grained level. Thus direct design of computing circuits might be impossible. In such situations an opportunistic approach to outsourcing computation can be adopted. The system is perturbed via two or more input loci and its dynamics if recorded at one or more output loci. A spike appearing at one of the output loci is interpreted as logical Truth or '1' and absence of the spike as logical False or '0'. Thus a system with relatively unknown structure implements a mapping $\{0, 1\}^n \rightarrow \{0, 1\}^m$, where n is a number of input loci and m is a number of output loci, $n, m > 0$. Using numerical modelling of excitation wavefronts propagating on images of real colony of *Aspergillus niger* we have demonstrated how sets of logical gates can be implemented in single colony mycelium networks via initiation of electrical impulses.[15] The impulses travel in the network, interact with each other (annihilate, reflect, change their phase). Thus for different combinations of input impulses and record different combinations of output impulses, which in some cases can be interpreted as representing two-inputs-one-output functions. To estimate a speed of computation we refer to Olsson and Hansson's original study,[16] in which they proposed that electrical activity in fungi could be used for communication

with message propagation speed 0.5 mm/sec. Diameter of the colony, which experimental laboratory images have been used to run the model, is *c.* 1.7 mm. Thus, it takes the excitation waves initiated at a boundary of the colony up to 3-4 sec to span the whole mycelium network (this time is equivalent to *c.* 70K iterations of the numerical integration model). In 3-4 sec the mycelium network can compute up to a hundred logical gates. This gives us the rate of a gate per 0.03 sec, or, in terms of frequency, this will be *c.* 30 Hz.

Programmability

To program fungal computers we must control the geometry of mycelium network. The geometry of mycelium network can be modified by varying nutritional conditions and temperature, especially a degree of branching is proportional to concentration of nutrients, and a wide range of chemical and physical stimuli. Also, we can geometrically constrain it. A feasibility of shaping similar networks has been demonstrated by us previously: high amplitude high frequency voltage applied between two electrodes in a network of protoplasmic tubes of slime mould *P. polycephalum* leads to abandonment of the stimulated protoplasmic without affecting the non stimulated tubes, and low amplitude low frequency voltage applied between two electrodes in the network enhance the stimulated tube and encourages abandonment of other tubes.

Application domain: distributed networks of ecological sensors

Likely application domains of the fungal devices could be large-scale networks of mycelium which collect and analyse information about the environment of soil and, possibly, air, and execute some decision making procedures. Fungi sense light, chemicals, gases, gravity and electric fields. Fungi show a pronounced response to changes in a substrate pH, demonstrate mechanosensing; they sense toxic metals, CO_2 and direction of fluid flow. Fungi exhibit thigmotactic and thigmomorphogenetic responses, which might be reflected in dynamic patterns of their electrical activity. Fungi are also capable of sensing chemical cues, especially stress hormones, from other species, thus they might be used as reporters of health and well-being of other inhabitants of the forest. Thus, fungal computers can be made an essential part of distributed large-scale environmental sensor networks in ecological research to assess not just soil quality but an over health of the ecosystems. Interaction of voltage spikes, travelling along mycelium strands, at the junctions between strands is a key mechanism of the fungal computation. We can see each junction as an elementary processor of a distributed multiprocessor computing network. We assume a number of junctions is proportional to a number of hyphal tips. There are estimated 10-20 tips per 1.5-3 mm^3 of a substrate. Without knowing the depth of the mycelial network we go for a safest lower margin of 2D estimation: 50 tips/mm^2. Considering that the largest known fungus *Armillaria bulbosa* populates over 15 hectares we could assume that there could be $75 \cdot 10^{17}$ branching points, that is nearly a trillion of elementary processing units. With regards to a speed of computation by fungal computers, electrical activity in fungi could be used for communication with message propagation speed 0.5 mm/sec (this is several orders slower than speed of a typical action potential

Fig. 6. Irina Perova, *The X-Files. Ecological Disaster in an Industrial Wonderland.* Installation with *Macrolepiota procera* fungi, 2020.

in plants: from 0.005 m/sec to 0.2 m/sec). Thus it would take about half-an-hour for a signal in the fungal computer to propagate one meter. The low speed of signal propagation is not a critical disadvantage of potential fungal computers, because they never meant to compete with conventional silicon devices. The mycelium network computing can not compete with existing silicon architecture however its application domain can be a unique of living biosensors (a distribution of gates realised might be affected by environmental conditions) and computation embedded into structural elements where fungal materials are used[18] and fungal wearables.[19]

[1] Professor in Unconventional Computing and Director of the Unconventional Computing, Lab, UWE, Bristol, UK.

[2] Affiliated artist in the Unconventional Computing, Lab, UWE, Bristol, UK.

[3] A. ADAMATZKY (ed.), *Advances in Unconventional Computing*, Cham, Springer, 2016.

[4] A. ADAMATZKY (ed.), *Advances in Physarum Machines*, Cham, Springer, 2016.

[5] C. L. SLAYMAN, W. S. LONG and D. GRADMANN, "'Action potentials' in Neurospora crassa, a mycelial fungus," *Biochimica et Biophysica Acta (BBA)-Biomembranes 426(4)*, 1976, 732-744.

[6] S. OLSSON & B. S. HANSSON, "Action potential-like activity found in fungal mycelia is sensitive to stimulation," *Naturwissenschaften 82(1)*, 1995, 30-31.

[7] A. ADAMATZKY, "On spiking behaviour of oyster fungi Pleurotus djamor," *Scientific reports 8(1)*, 2018, 1-7.

[8] A. ADAMATZKY (ed.), *Advances in Physarum Machines, op. cit.*

[9] J. FROMM & S. LAUTNER, "Electrical signals and their physiological significance in plants," *Plant, cell & environment 30(3)*, 2007, 249-257.

[10] A. ADAMATZKY, "On spiking behaviour of oyster fungi Pleurotus djamor," *op. cit.*

[11] A. E. BEASLEY, A. L. POWELL and A. ADAMATZKY, "Memristive properties of mushrooms," arXiv preprint arXiv:2002.06413 (2020).

[12] *Ibid.*

[13] A. ADAMATZKY, G. GANDIA and A. CHIOLERIO, "Fungal sensing skin," arXiv preprint arXiv:2008.09814 (2020).

[14] J. MITCHELL, G. GANDIA, J. SABU and A. BISMARCK, "Leather-like material biofabrication using fungi," *Nature Sustainability*, 2020, 1-8.

[15] A. ADAMATZKY, M. TEGELAAR, H. A. WOSTEN, A. L. POWELL, A. E. BEASLEY, and R. MAYNE, "On Boolean gates in fungal colony," *Biosystems*, 2020, 104138.

[16] S. OLSSON & B. S. HANSSON, "Action potential-like activity found in fungal mycelia is sensitive to stimulation," *op. cit.*

[17] A. E. BEASLEY, A. L. POWELL and A. ADAMATZKY, "Capacitive storage in mycelium substrate," arXiv preprint arXiv:2003.07816 (2020).

[18] A. ADAMATZKY, P. AYRES, G. BELOTTI and H. A. WÖSTEN, "Fungal Architecture Position Paper," *International Journal of Unconventional Computing 14*, 2019.

[19] A. ADAMATZKY, A. NIKOLAIDOU, A. GANDIA, A. CHIOLERIO, and M. M. DEHSHIB, "Reactive fungal wearable," arXiv preprint arXiv:2009.05670 (2020).

Le vignoble cosmique

Alessandro Chiolerio[1]

Gianni Verna, « Digradano su noi pendici / di basse vigne », gravure sur bois, 1360x480 mm, 1991.

Tout est si ouvert, même à la pluie poussée par le vent et aux rayons clairs du soleil, tout est aussi silencieux que le regard du spectateur, seul un spectateur patient pourrait voir un outil poussiéreux, un reste de guerre très bruyant, ou un tracteur moderne brillant, une créature technologique parcourir les rangs.

Pourtant, cette même technologie pourrait nous aider à voir une colline d'une manière différente, le vignoble reposant harmonieusement dessus, la plantation ordonnée des vignes, leur production de sucre obstinée, enfin savamment transformée en or rouge liquide. Le vignoble étant constamment soumis aux champs électromagnétiques naturels, aux signaux radio que les étoiles nous envoient. Ce chuchotement électrique polarise nos vignes, se disperse dans une symphonie d'impulsions, détermine leur métabolisme, peut-être leur humeur. Et qu'affinons-nous sinon leur humeur, à l'aide d'enzymes et de bactéries, pour en faire du vin ? Le vin est le résultat de ce calcul de proportions cosmiques et holistiques, qui finit par nous envahir et nous enivrer d'étincelles d'étoiles.

La complexité d'une vigne

La vigne se développe au fil des saisons, par la fatigue et le travail du paysan. Mais on cache beaucoup de secrets invisibles. La vigne a une histoire fascinante, qui accompagne l'histoire de l'homme et de ses migrations depuis des millénaires. Des découvertes récentes montrent que la production de vin est documentée à partir du VIe millénaire avant J.-C. dans des endroits très éloignés les uns des autres, comme le Caucase[2], la Sicile[3] et la Sardaigne[4] (Fig. 1). La production de vin était si importante que lorsque l'épidémie de phylloxéra a détruit la plupart des vignobles européens, on a appris à créer des chimères avec les vignes américaines les plus résistantes. Et une partie de cette histoire reste à écrire, car de nouveaux hybrides résistants aux maladies sont en cours de développement pour assurer un avenir durable à nos vignerons[5].

Un vignoble est un système extrêmement complexe dans lequel les principales espèces

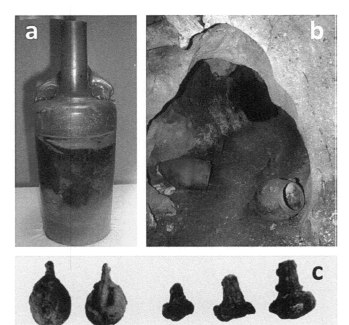

Fig. 1. a : La bouteille de vin de Speyer, datée d'environ 325-359 après J.-C., trouvée lors des fouilles d'une villa patricienne romaine et conservée au Musée historique du Palatinat, en Allemagne (photo d'Emmanuel Giel) ; c'est le plus ancien échantillon de vin qui nous soit parvenu. b: bocaux B1 et B2 trouvés dans le tunnel Bellitti à Monte Kronio, Sciacca (Sicile), contenant des traces d'acide tartrique et de tartrate de sodium ; ils remontent au début de l'âge du cuivre, environ 4000 avant J.-C. c: graines de raisins domestiques, *Vitis vinifera* subsp. *Vinifera* et pédicelles, trouvés dans un puits de Villanovan près de Bologne, environ 900 avant JC.

Fig. 2. a : Association de *Orchis purpurea* et *Ranunculus acris* avec *Vitis vinifera*. b : Association de *Taraxacum officinale* avec *Vitis vinifera*. c : Association de *Muscari neglectum* avec *Vitis vinifera*. d : Association de *Viola odorata* avec *Vitis vinifera*. Les vignobles sur les photos sont situés sur le territoire de la commune de Vigliano d'Asti.

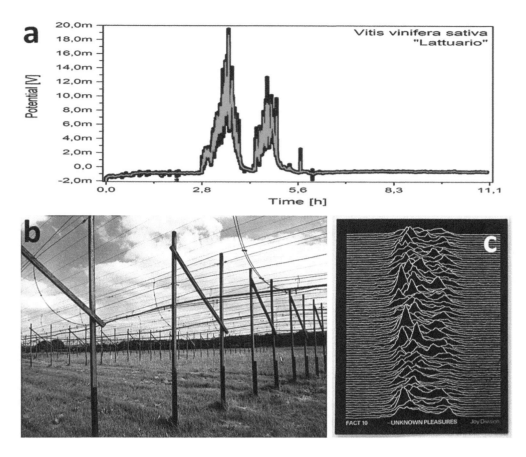

Fig. 3. a : Exemple de pic de potentiel bioélectrique enregistré pendant les heures de nuit par une vigne Lattuario à Turin, en 2020. b : Interplanetary Scintillation Array (ISA) à l'Observatoire de radioastronomie Mullard, archives photographiques du Département de physique, Université de Cambridge (1967). c: couverture de l'album Unknown Pleasures de Joy Division (1979). Bien qu'il fasse désormais partie de l'imaginaire collectif, peu savent qu'il ne s'agit pas de traces sonores, mais du radiogramme original enregistré par Jocelyn Bell Burnell et Antony Hewish, deux astronomes du Mullard, qui en cherchant des traces de quasars ont découvert le premier signal pulsar, l'appelant LGM-1 (Little Green Man-1, aujourd'hui il s'appelle CP1919), représenté par Harold Craft, un étudiant de l'Université Cornell et pionnier de la visualisation de données numériques.

peuvent vivre des dizaines voire des centaines d'années, les racines s'étendant jusqu'à cinq mètres à l'horizontal et à un mètre à la verticale, créant une symbiose au fil des ans avec de nombreuses espèces de bactéries et de champignons, collaborant avec des herbes au développement de la chimie des sols (Fig. 2). Un nombre incalculable d'espèces animales coexistent alors avec les vignes, la plupart sont des insectes et des arachnides, qui entrelacent leur vie et leur mort à l'enchevêtrement de tissus de soie, de fils de fer et de feuilles de vigne séchées.

Influx qui vient des étoiles

Un vignoble est naturellement exposé à l'environnement extérieur et en tant que tel, il absorbe les radiations électromagnétiques, le flux de particules chargées, les neutrinos, les rayons cosmiques, qui interagissent faiblement avec la matière ordinaire. Cette interaction est aussi sporadique que cruciale pour l'écologie de notre planète. Un exemple frappant est représenté par les processus qui régissent la condensation d'un nuage. Les noyaux de condensation porteurs d'une charge électrique subissent en effet une croissance spontanée pour former les gouttelettes d'eau qui constituent un nuage. Et il n'y a aucun doute que les rayons cosmiques y jouent un rôle fondamental[6]. Un organisme vivant, qu'il soit végétal ou animal, est sensible à toutes les conditions extérieures auxquelles il est soumis ; il est possible d'extrapoler des informations à son sujet, par exemple en surveillant le potentiel bioélectrique de cet organisme. L'étude et l'analyse numérique des potentiels d'action pourraient, entre autres, permettre de surveiller la santé d'une culture, ce qui est essentiel pour prévenir l'apparition et la propagation d'agents pathogènes contre lesquels les vignerons luttent perpétuellement pour sauvegarder la production agricole, comme le mildiou et l'oïdium. De plus, en « écoutant » la pensée des vignes, nous avons pu collecter suffisamment de données pour déterminer leur bien-être émotionnel, et mettre en œuvre des actions visant à les faire se sentir mieux, afin que la qualité des raisins, et par conséquent du vin, soit affectée positivement. Par exemple par l'expérimentation musicale et sonore[7]. Et peut-être découvrira-t-on qu'ils se comportent comme un organisme collectif[8] !

Le vent solaire mis en bouteille

La scintillation interplanétaire est la variation de l'intensité d'une source radio cosmique, caractérisée par un très petit diamètre d'émission, induite par des fluctuations de l'indice de réfraction du milieu interplanétaire turbulent. Les perturbations de la phase du front d'onde, qui peuvent être supposées parallèles à la surface de la Terre, proviennent de la diffraction qui produit de petites inhomogénéités dans la densité électronique du milieu, qui sont finalement directement proportionnelles à la densité du vent solaire. Cette diffraction peut à son tour être corrélée à des changements brusques de la vitesse du vent solaire, ou à des événements particulièrement énergétiques tels que l'éjection de masse coronale du Soleil. Un instrument capable de mesurer la scintillation interplanétaire pendant 24 heures est donc un analyseur de l'héliosphère interne, qui fournit des informations très utiles relatives à la météorologie spatiale[9], à même de nous aider à préserver nos systèmes électroniques et de télécommunication devenus désormais fondamentaux, notamment suite au développement de la pandémie. Comment cet instrument est-il fabriqué ? À tous égards semblable à un vignoble (Fig. 3), constitué de longs fils métalliques conducteurs, et éventuellement de nombreuses rangées placées dans des positions à différentes longueurs[10], pouvant cartographier le ciel alors qu'il coule devant leurs yeux pour intégrer les fluctuations locales de la densité ionosphérique au fil du temps et les annuler. Quel meilleur outil qu'un vignoble ? Le radiotélescope fonctionnerait à des fréquences comprises entre 50 et 500 MHz, en fonction de ses caractéristiques de construction : la longueur des fils de réception détermine uniquement la tonalité sur laquelle vous syntonisez. Et il ne serait pas affecté par les signaux bioélectriques des vignes, qui suivent des processus physiologiques beaucoup plus lents et plus proches du Courant Continu.

En substance, la construction d'une usine expérimentale permettrait aux agriculteurs de disposer d'un nouvel outil d'analyse de l'état de bien-être du vignoble, aux scientifiques d'un nouvel outil de mesure de la scintillation interplanétaire, et aux consommateurs de boire un vin tracé, où les techniques modernes de la blockchain et de l'IoT convergeraient pour compiler un passeport numérique contenant les notes de la symphonie cosmique qui a secoué le vignoble pendant toute une année. En effet, grâce à la blockchain, il est possible de stocker des informations par ordre chronologique concernant la période de temps pendant laquelle les transformations du vin ont eu lieu, du champ à la bouteille. Les systèmes IoT, d'autre part, peuvent être utilisés pour collecter sur le terrain les paramètres climatologiques environnementaux tels que la pression, la température, l'humidité relative, l'humidité du sol, la vitesse et la direction du vent, le degré d'ensoleillement, l'humidité des feuilles, *etc.*, et transmettre ces informations via des canaux sans fil à un système capable de les mémoriser. Toutes ces données contribueraient donc à la formation du passeport numérique du vin en question.

[1] Istituto Italiano di Tecnologia, Center for Sustainable Future Technologies, Via Livorno 30, 10144 Turin, Italie ; University of West of England, Unconventional Computing Lab, Coldharbour Lane, BS16 1QY Bristol, Royaume-Uni.

[2] D. LORDKIPANIDZE, « Le antichissime origini della viticoltura in Georgia », in G. DI PASQUALE (éd.), *Vinum Nostrum, arte, scienza e miti del vino nelle civiltà del Mediterraneo antico. Catalogo della mostra (Firenze 20 juillet 2010 - 30 avril 2011)*, Florence, Giunti, 2010, 32-33.

[3] D. TANASI, E. GRECO, V. DI TULLIO, D. CAPITANI, D. GULLÌ, E. CILIBERTO, « H-1H NMR 2D-TOCSY, ATR FT-IR and SEM-EDX for the identification of organic residues on Sicilian prehistoric pottery », *Micromechanical Journal 135*, 2017, 140-147.

[4] M. RUBINO, « Sardo, rosso, di 3mila anni fa: identikit del vino più antico del Mediterraneo », *La Repubblica online*, https://www.repubblica.it/sapori/2016/12/19/news/sardegna_primo_vino_millenario-154444878/.

[5] R. TESTOLIN, E. PETERLUNGER, S. COLLOVINI, S. CASTELLARIN, G. DI GASPERO, F. ANACLERIO, M. COLAUTTI, M. DE CANDIDO, E. DE LUCA, A. KHAFIZOVA, et E. SARTORI, « Le varietà resistenti alle malattie », *Quaderni tecnici VCR, 18 (3e édition)*, 2018.

[6] J. KIRKBY *et alii*, « Role of sulphuric acid, ammonia and galactic cosmic rays in atmospheric aerosol nucléation », *Nature 476*, 2011, 429.

[7] Ş. PETRESCU, R. MUSTĂŢEA, I. NICORICI, « The influence of music on seed germination of Beta vulgaris l. var. Cicla l. », *Journal of Young Scientist V*, 2017, 67-72.

[8] V. ZAPPALÀ, *Vini dell'altro mondo*, Il mio libro, 2012.

[9] J. A. GONZÁLEZ-ESPARZA, A. CARRILLO, E. ANDRADE, R. PÉREZ ENRÍQUEZ et S. KURTZ, « The MEXART interplanetary scintillation array in Mexico », *Geofísica International 43(1)*, 2004, 61-73.

[10] M. TOKUMARU, M. KOJIMA, K. FUJIKI, K. MARUYAMA, Y. MARUYAMA, H. ITO, et T. IJU, « A newly developed UHF radiotelescope for interplanetary scintillation observations: Solar Wind Imaging Facility », *Radio Science 46*, 2011, RSoFo2.

Novel reversible logic elements for unconventional computing

Kenichi Morita[1]

Logic elements used in conventional computers are mostly logic gates such as AND, OR, NOT, NAND, etc. Their history is quite long, since logical operations of AND, OR and NOT were already known more than two-thousand years ago.[2] They were obtained by analyzing human thinking and reasoning, and thus it is easy for us to understand them. However, when we investigate future computing systems, we should not be tied to the old traditions. Reversible computing[3] is a paradigm of computing that reflects physical reversibility, one of the fundamental microscopic physical laws of nature. It searches for novel and unconventional methodologies that are directly related to reversible microscopic phenomena. We consider here a reversible logic element with 1-bit memory (RLEM), and examine its possibilities as a novel logical device. Though its physical realizability in the nano-level is not known at present, it gives new vistas on unconventional computing devices. We shall see that it has very different features that cannot be seen in conventional logic gates. In particular, reversible computing systems such as reversible Turing machines can be constructed out of RLEMs in a very unique way. We also see that an RLEM can be implemented in reversible environments such as a billiard ball model of computation, and a very simple reversible cellular automaton. In the following, these features are explained using many illustrations without giving technical details.

Reversible logic element with 1-bit memory

A *reversible logic element with 1-bit memory* (RLEM) is a kind of reversible finite automaton. Fig. 1 shows a typical example of an RLEM with four input ports and four output ports called a *rotary element* (RE).[4] Conceptually, it has a rotatable bar that controls the move direction of an incoming signal (or a particle). It takes one of the two states H and V depending on the direction of the bar (*i.e.*, horizontal or vertical). If a signal comes from the direction parallel to the bar, it goes straight ahead and the state does not change. If a signal comes from the direction orthogonal to the bar, it turns rightward and the state changes. It is reversible in the following sense: From the state at $t+1$ and the output, the state at t and the input are uniquely determined.

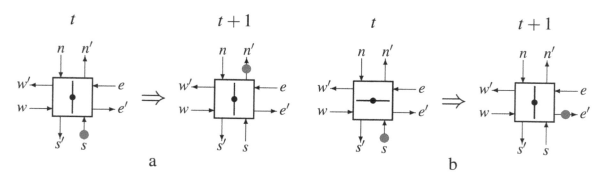

Fig. 1. Rotary element (RE) and its operations. (a) The parallel case, and (b) the orthogonal case.

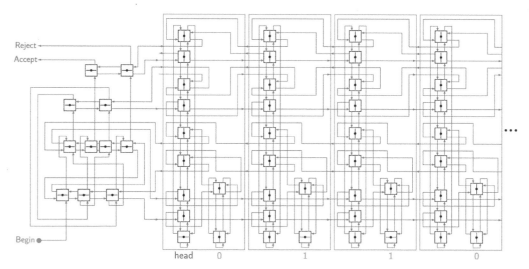

Fig. 2. An example of a reversible Turing machine composed of rotary elements.

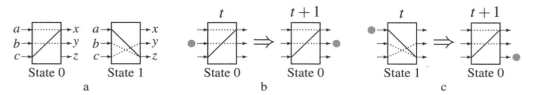

Fig. 3. (a) Two states of RLEM 3-7. (b) The case where the state does not change. (c) The case where the state changes.

Composing reversible computers out of rotary elements

A *reversible Turing machine* is an abstract model of a reversible computer where every computational state has at most one predecessor. Hence, we can trace back its computing process uniquely. It is known that any (irreversible) Turing machine can be simulated by reversible one without leaving garbage information on the tape, and thus reversible Turing machines are computationally universal.[5] We can construct any reversible Turing machine out of rotary elements. Fig. 2 shows a circuit that simulates a simple reversible Turing machine that checks if a unary number given on its tape is even.[6] In this figure, a finite-state control of the reversible Turing machine is in the left part, and a tape unit is in the right part. If a particle is given to the Begin port, it starts to compute.

Universal RLEMs

There are infinitely many RLEMs if we do not restrict the number of input/output ports. Fig. 3 shows RLEM No. 3-7, where "3" stands for 3-input and 3-output, and "7" is its serial number. Two boxes in Fig. 3(a) indicate its two states. The dotted and solid lines give input-output relation in each state. If an input signal goes through a dotted line, the state does not change (Fig. 3(b)). If it goes through a solid line, the state changes (Fig. 3(c)). Note that RE can also be represented by such a figure, but we employ Fig. 1 for ease in understanding. An RLEM is called *universal* if it can simulate any other RLEM. Remarkably, it has been proved that *every* RLEM (except degenerate ones) is universal if it has three or more input/ output ports.[7] Therefore, RLEM 3-7 and RE are of course universal. Figure 4 shows how to simulate an RE by RLEM 3-7. Replacing each occurrence of REs in Fig. 2 by the circuit of Fig. 4, we obtain

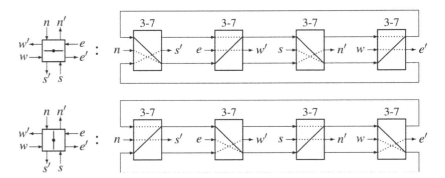

Fig. 4. Simulating a rotary element by a circuit composed of RLEM 3-7.

Fig. 5. A rotary element realized in the billiard ball model, an idealized mechanical computing model.

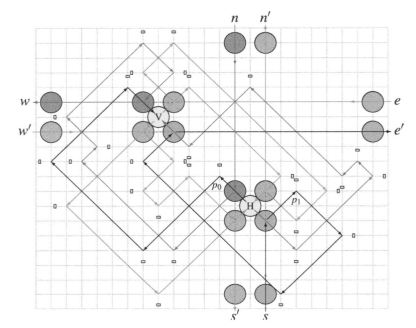

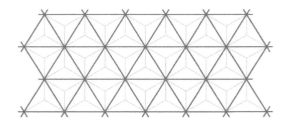

Fig. 6. Cellular space of an elementary triangular partitioned cellular automaton (ETPCA).

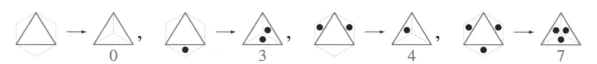

Fig. 7. Local transition rules of ETPCA 0347.

a circuit made of RLEM 3-7 that simulates the reversible Turing machine.

Simulating a rotary element using billiard balls

The *billiard ball model* (BBM) of computation was proposed by Edward Fredkin and Tommaso Toffoli[8] to show that the Fredkin gate, a universal reversible logic gate, is realizable in the BBM. It is a kind of reversible mechanical system consisting of ideal elastic balls and reflectors. We can see that an RE is also realized in the BBM as shown in Fig. 5, where small rectangles are reflectors.[9] Here, two kinds of balls, *i.e.*, a *state ball* and a *signal ball*, are used. One of the key points of the construction is that the state ball (yellow) is put stationarily at the position H or V in a resting mode. Fig. 5 shows the cases where the directions of the bar and the incoming signal are orthogonal as in Fig. 1(b). Consider the case that the state ball is put at the position H, and the signal ball (green) comes from the input port s. The signal ball collides with the state ball at the position H. Then, the state ball and the signal ball move along the paths p_0 and p_1, respectively. When the state ball comes to the position V, these balls collide again. Then, the state ball stops at V, while the signal ball moves eastward and goes out from the output port e'. By this the operation of Fig. 1(b) is realized. The case that the state ball is at the position V, and the signal ball comes from s is trivial. In this case, the signal ball simply moves northward without interacting with the state ball and the reflectors, and thus Fig. 1(a) is realized. In this way, the whole circuit that simulates a reversible Turing machine given in Fig. 2 is also embeddable in the BBM.

Realizing RLEMs in a simple reversible cellular space

There is yet another spatiotemporal model of a reversible environment called a *reversible cellular automaton*. A cellular automaton (CA) consists of an infinite number of finite automata called *cells* that are placed and connected uniformly in a space. A cell changes its state depending on the states of its neighboring cells. We use a special type of a CA called an *elementary triangular partitioned cellular automaton* (ETPCA) since it is very simple. Each cell of ETPCA is triangular, and it is further divided into three parts (Fig. 6). Each part has two states 0 and 1, which are indicated by a blank and a dot. Here, we consider a particular local transition function defined by the four local transition rules shown in Fig. 7, which is identified by the number 0347.[10] We assume that these rules are rotation-symmetric, *i.e.*, for each rule in Fig. 7 there exist rules obtained by rotating both sides of it by a multiple of 60 degrees. As seen from Fig. 7, the next state of a cell is determined by the three parts of its neighboring cells.

Consider the configuration given at time $t=0$ in Fig. 8. Applying the local function to all the cells in parallel, we have a configuration at $t=1$. Configurations at $t=2,3,...$ are obtained likewise. Note that, the dot patterns at $t=0$ and $t=6$ are the same except that the latter is shifted rightward. Hence, it is a space-moving pattern called a *glider*, which can be used as a signal. The local transition function defined by the rules in Fig. 7 is injective, since there is no pair of distinct rules whose right-hand sides are the same. By this, for each configuration we can find a previous configuration uniquely. Such an ETPCA is called *reversible*.

The moving direction of a glider is controlled by a stable pattern called a *block*. Figure 9 shows the process of the backward turn by a single block. At $t=0$ a glider (left) is about to collide a block (right). At $t=38$ the glider is split into a *rotator* (left) and a *fin* (right). The fin moves around the block. At $t=97$ the rotator and the fin meet, and a glider is reconstructed. Then the resulting glider moves leftward. Appropriately placing several blocks, we can also realize the right turn by 120 degrees, the left turn by 120 degrees, and the U-turn of a glider.

Combining several useful phenomena found in the reversible cellular space of ETPCA 0347, we can construct a pattern that simulates RLEM 3-7 (Fig. 3) as shown in Fig. 10. A glider is given to one of the three input ports as a signal. After changing the state, the glider

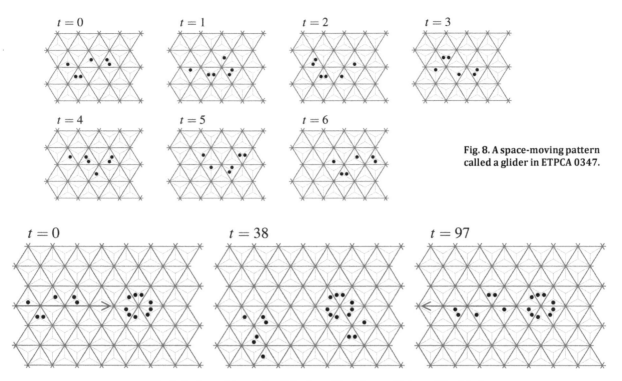

Fig. 8. A space-moving pattern called a glider in ETPCA 0347.

Fig. 9. Backward turn of a glider is realized by a collision with a block.

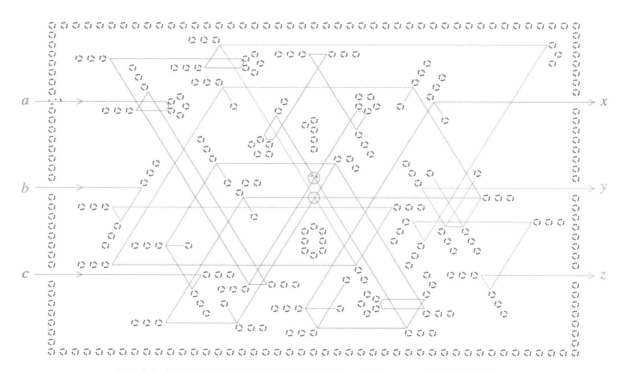

Fig. 10. RLEM 3-7 implemented in the reversible cellular space of ETPCA 0347.

comes out from one of the output ports. The pattern contains many backward turn, right turn, and U-turn modules. To keep the state of RLEM 3-7, a fin is put around the center of the pattern. A fin is a periodic pattern of period 6 consisting of three dots. Two small circles in the figure show possible positions of a fin. If a fin is at the lower (upper, respectively) position, then we consider the state is 0 (1). Testing whether the fin is at the position 0 or 1, and shifting it between these two positions are performed by collisions of the glider. In this way, RLEM 3-7 is simulated in the cellular space of ETPCA 0347 having an extremely simple local function. Since a rotary element can be composed of RLEM 3-7, circuits that simulate reversible Turing machines like the one in Fig. 2 are also simulated in this cellular space. An emulator for ETPCA 0347 has been given,[11] which works on the general purpose cellular automaton simulator *Golly*.[12] There, computing processes of reversible Turing machines composed of RLEM 4-31 can be seen.

[1] Proffessor Emeritus, Hiroshima University, Higashi-Hiroshima, Japan.

[2] J. M. BOCHENSKI, *Ancient Formal Logic*, Amsterdam, North-Holland, 1951.

[3] K. MORITA, *Theory of Reversible Computing*, Tokyo, Springer, 2017.

[4] K. MORITA, "A simple reversible logic element and cellular automata for reversible computing," in M. MARGENSTERN & Y. ROGOZHIN (eds), *Proceedings of MCU (International Conference on Machines, Computations, and Universality) 2001, LNCS 2055*, Berlin, Heidelberg, Springer, 2001, 102-113.

[5] C. H. BENNETT, "Logical reversibility of computation," *IBM J. Res. Dev. 17*, 1973, 525-532.

[6] K. MORITA, "Constructing reversible Turing machines by reversible logic element with memory," in A. ADAMATZKY (ed.), *Automata, Universality, Computation*, Cham, Springer, 2015, 127-138. Hiroshima University Institutional Repository, http://ir.lib.hiroshima-u.ac.jp/00029224 (2010).

[7] K. MORITA, T. OGIRO, A. ALHAZOV, and T. TANIZAWA, "Non-degenerate 2-state reversible logic elements with three or more symbols are all universal," *Journal of Multiple-Valued Logic and Soft Computing 18*, 2010, 37-54.

[8] E. FREDKIN & T. TOFFOLI, "Conservative logic," *International Journal of Theoretical Physics 21*, 1982, 219-253.

[9] K. MORITA, *Theory of Reversible Computing*, op. cit.

[10] K. MORITA, "A universal non-conservative reversible elementary triangular partitioned cellular automaton that shows complex behavior," *Natural Computing 18(3)*, 2019, 413-428.

[11] K. MORITA, "Reversible world: Data set for simulating a reversible elementary triangular partitioned cellular automaton on Golly," Hiroshima University Institutional Repository, http://ir.lib.hiroshima-u.ac.jp/00042655 (2017).

[12] A. TREVORROW, T. ROKICKI, T. HUTTON *et al*, "Golly: an open source, cross-platform application for exploring Conway's Game of Life and other cellular automata," http://golly.sourceforge.net/ (2005).

An Unconventional Look at AI: Why Today's Machine Learning Systems are not Intelligent

Nancy Salay[1]

Machine learning systems (MLS) that model low-level processes are the cornerstones of current AI systems. These 'indirect' learners are good at classifying kinds that are distinguished solely by their manifest physical properties. But the more a kind is a function of spatio-temporally extended properties — words, situation-types, social norms — the less likely an MLS will be able to track it. Systems that can interact with objects at the individual level, on the other hand, and that can sustain this interaction, can learn responses to increasingly abstract properties, including representational ones. This representational capacity, arguably the mark of intelligence, then, is not available to current MLS's.

Introduction

The current rhetoric has it that AI is here, or, at least, around the corner. But if this claim is false, then treating systems as such, that is, relying on them to make judgements, could have grave consequences. Autonomous vehicles are just one example of the many new AI technologies poised to enter the public space. Since stemming this technological tide seems futile, the academy has a responsibility to raise the public's understanding around what constitutes intelligence. Here I begin this effort by arguing that we should stop thinking about current machine learning systems (MLS's) as 'intelligences' since they do not model the learning necessary for intelligent behaviour.

What is Intelligent Behaviour?

The very first question we might ask, then, is "What is it to act intelligently?" Examples help orient our thinking so let us begin with a few here. A robot that has been programmed to perform basic household chores, but which freezes when confronted with an unfamiliar task or situation, is not behaving intelligently: it can do only what it has been programmed to do. Similarly, any machine that does only what the limits of its design permit and no more — *calculators, toasters, cranes* — does so without what we would call intelligence. In contrast, beings who make novel responses to novel situations, who 'figure out' what to

do next, provide us with paradigmatic intelligent behaviour. Think here of the battery of researchers currently working on the problem of developing a Covid-19 vaccine. The task draws on much background knowledge, to be sure, but it also requires a capacity for solving new kinds of problems. If we were not confident that these scientists were capable of such 'out-of-the-box' thinking, we'd have no reason for hope.

But we need to be careful — a novel response is not always an indicator of an intelligent response. Many animals are capable of adapting to changing situations in what seem like 'pre-programmed' ways: viruses mutate when hosts become resistant; cockroaches change food sources during resource scarcity; and, primates shift their group dynamics when territories diminish. We call the capacity for this sort of behavioural change 'adaptability.' While there is a relationship between adaptability and intelligence — they are both capacities for learning new responses to new situations — the former is on an evolutionary time-scale, one that extends across individuals to species, and the latter is on a developmental time-scale, one that extends across an individual over its own lifetime. From the perspective of the individual, adaptive responses are canned responses, backup strategies that kick in when first pass responses fail; only from the perspective of the species are such responses novel. Intelligent responses, in contrast, are local strategies that individuals develop in response to new, locally experienced, situations.

Intelligent Action is not Continual

Notice that having a capacity for intelligent action does not entail that one uses this capacity all the time. That it does was the working assumption in the early days of AI — 'Good-Old-Fashioned-AI' (GOFAI). On those completely top-down models, every action (limited to simple screen outputs in most cases since GOFAI systems were not equipped with bodies) was the product of a line of 'reasoning,' a decision. Today, thanks to the insights of Embodied Cognitive Science and, more broadly, Phenomenology, we understand that even intelligent individuals mostly act in automatic or unconsciously directed ways. Such actions might be skillful, as when someone plays an instrument or adeptly traverses a narrow cliff-side path, but such behaviour unfolds according to learned responses to the occurrent features of an ongoing situation. When an obstacle looms, the body swivels to avoid it; when a note is played, the next note in the learned sequence is anticipated. In intelligent behaviour, in contrast, factors beyond the occurrent features of the ongoing situation influence our behaviour: a note is played, but now the anticipated next note is not played. My musical execution of Beethoven's Emperor Concerto might be skillful, but when I intersperse it with the melodic line for Happy Birthday, because I know that today is yours, I have acted intelligently as well. That it is your birthday is not a physical fact in the occurrent situation in which we are participating and yet, as intelligent beings, it is something to which we are both capable of responding.

Representation makes Intelligent Behaviour Possible

How do we become responsive to such 'offline' factors? We represent them to ourselves and one another. A classic demonstration of the dramatic behavioural effect this capacity for representation can have is the infamous marshmallow test.[2] A subject, usually a child, is presented with a single marshmallow. He is told that he is welcome to eat it but, if he can sit patiently for X minutes without tasting the marshmallow, he will receive another marshmallow in addition to the first. He will receive one marshmallow if it is eaten right away and two marshmallows if he waits until the experimenter returns. Young children find it very difficult to resist the sensory draw of the marshmallow and generally give in and eat it before the experimenter returns. As children mature, however, they are increasingly able to wait for the arrival of the second marshmallow. They are capable of suffering through short term deprivation — not tasting the marshmallow that is present — for the sake of increased future gain — two marshmallows. To repeatedly not succumb to the marshmallow temptation, to what is sensorily present, children must behave now in a way that takes into account factors that are not spatio-temporally present, namely that there is a potential for future gain. Younger children, perhaps because they have not developed the relevant linguistic representational skills, are capable only of responding to the occurrent, sensory factors of the situation. Being thus completely in the moment, they gobble up the sweet-smelling treat. Another version of the marshmallow experiment,[3] this time a reverse contingency test with chimpanzee subjects, demonstrates the critical role of representations in intelligent behaviour even more clearly. A chimpanzee is presented with two plates of treats, one having visibly more than the other, and is invited to choose one of them. A second chimp sits by, observing. The plate chosen is given to the second chimp and the chooser is awarded the one not selected. Similarly to young children, though they understand the terms of the offer perfectly well, chimpanzees are incapable of resisting the overwhelming sensory draw of the treats — *their smell, touch, appearance* — and they invariably choose the plate with the greatest amount. Repeatedly they watch, furiously, as the larger pile of candies goes to the lucky bystander. But when a slightly altered version of the experiment was run with a chimpanzee — *Sheba* — who already knew some rudimentary mathematical symbols, the results were very different. Instead of being asked to choose between two plates with visible piles of candies, Sheba was offered two plates with lids labelled with the number of treats underneath. Since numbers have no sensory draw whatever, Sheba was now able to consistently make the self-maximising choice of the plate with fewer candies. By using the numbers, representing the possibility of future treats, Sheba was able to take into consideration factors that were not spatio-temporally present and thereby make the intelligent choice.

Representations have Unusual Properties

A word needs to be said here about representations themselves since they are peculiar things. A representation — for example, a sentence utterance, a physical token such as a game playing piece, or an occurrent thought — has, in addition to the usual physical properties that all physical things have, representational properties that extend beyond these. My arm is a configuration of cells and impulses, and this is all that it is, nothing more than these physical properties. But the sentence token, "My arm is a configuration of cells and impulses," has the physical properties constituted by the ink on this page, the molecules in the paper, and so on, as well as the property of being about my arm. It represents the world, with respect to my arm at least, as being a certain way. The technical term for this property of representation is 'intentionality:' anything that is about something beyond itself in this way is an intentional thing. All signs,[4] then – words and sentences, numbers, icons – are intentional objects. And if we think that thoughts are internal representations of the way the world is or could be, then they are intentional objects as well.

Unlike physical properties, however, representational properties are not intrinsic to things. A stop sign is a symbol in the context of road traffic systems, but outside of these contexts, to a squirrel for example, the stop sign is merely a physical thing in the world, representing nothing. Likewise, the sentence "My arm is a configuration of cells and impulses," to someone who does not speak English or to something not capable of speaking at all is just the physical thing that it is, the letter-shaped ink patterns on the page, representing nothing. Physical objects become symbols only in the context of a larger system within which individuals respond to them in ways that point beyond themselves. Such individuals are themselves intentional beings since they can respond to a symbol's representational properties as well as its physical ones. Intentionality, then, is a key aspect of intelligence.

To build an intentional machine, namely one that can use representations to guide its behaviour, is one of the central tasks of AI. The foundational assumption that continues to drive research in the field, and which has spawned the current zeitgeist of mainstream cognitive science more generally, is this: intentionality is (exhaustively) reducible to low-level processes. If we want to understand the intentional capacity of human beings, we need to look inside human beings, at their neural circuitry mostly, to see which aspects of it are responsible for intentional behaviour. In other words, the capacity to respond to a symbol's representational properties (and not just its physical ones) is nothing more than a (possibly very complex) combination of the low-level processes that constitute the response behaviour. The problem with this idea, however, is that it is wrong: low-level processes and personal-level intentional behaviour are not comparable, and hence not identifiable, activities. Yes, of course, the sub-personal processes of Fred taken together are necessary for Fred to learn a new language, but, they are not sufficient: factors that are external to Fred, e.g. the way that symbols are used in his linguistic community, determine whether and how Fred's learned responses are about anything at all, which is to say, whether they are intentional at all. Furthermore, a model of just the sub-personal learning part of Fred's linguistic skill, placed in the appropriate environment, will not yield the appropriate intentional behaviour. Without coordinated, personal-level activity, Fred's neural activity is just a series of low-level processes, not linguistic at all. In other words, intentional behaviour is a personal-level activity, not a low-level one. This is not a distinction that is often made in cognitive science, but it is a critical one in the context of artificial intelligence research. If intentionality is not exhaustively accounted for by sub-personal activity, then AI systems that only model sub-personal activity, which is precisely what current MLS's do, will not be intelligent. Here I will try, in broad brush strokes, to explain how and why low-level processes cannot constitute intentional behaviour.

Low-Level Processing is not Intentional

MLS's model, albeit simplistically, the low-level neural processes that underwrite organism learning. Today's MLS's have achieved much success in classification, in 'learning' to distinguish between different kinds of objects, pictures of cats and dogs, for example. I call this 'learning' in scare quotes because the relevant classifying behaviour is achieved only indirectly, by way of the pixel-level features that consistently corelate with object-level kinds such as dogs and cats. That there really are natural kinds in the world — individuals that share a statistically significant sub-set of features with other individuals — is what makes this kind of indirect learning useful. If the world were not regular in this way, if there were no natural kinds, such an approach would be useless. Imagine a world in which low-level patterns did not correspond to anything useful at the personal level, where a low-level sequence meant CAT one day and then DOG the next! This is an important factor to keep in mind: the learning success of indirect classifiers is partly determined by the high-level homogeneity of environmental conditions.

But given that our world *is* populated by dependable, statistical regularities, isn't this indirect learning good enough? For simple applications, in the context of web searches for example, it might be. As a model of personal-level behaviour, however, it falls short: there is a critical granularity gap between low-level processing and object-level action. At the low-level, interaction is with sensory bits — in the case of our example MLS these are pixels — not with medium-sized objects such as cats and dogs. One low-level processing time-step does not register at the object-level of granularity at all and, conversely, a single

action at the object-level corresponds to thousands of low-level processing steps. Relative to the object-level, processing occurs at speeds that do not register as activity at all; while, relative to the processing level, object-level change occurs so slowly that, again, it does not register as change at all during a single, low-level time-step. The two levels of granularity are thus spatio-temporally distinct. Since MLS's cannot interact directly with medium-sized objects, but only indirectly over many low-level time-steps and by way of regular, low-level features, the object 'learning' they achieve will always be brittle. Change one lower-level feature of an object that the MLS has not had training on, and it breaks. For this reason, no matter how robust the low-level training is, MLS's will always be subject to adversarial attack. But, more saliently with respect to the question of intelligence, such systems could never learn to respond to an object's representational properties. More on this momentarily. The only sense in which a cat/dog classifier represents a distinction between the concepts CAT and DOG is from our spatio-temporally extended vantage point relative to the network, namely the vantage point of the personal-level, from which we can see that the ongoing activity of the network corresponds to a distinction between cats and dogs. From the classifier's vantage point, however, there are only ever pixels and responses to them; there are no cats and dogs at all.

To help clarify what it is for an individual to interact and learn about an object directly, let us first consider another personal-level activity: locomotion. A cat jumps from the ground to a branch by virtue of a multitude of ongoing, low-level processes that constitute its personal-level activity, but none of the low-level processes are themselves locomotions. Locomotion is something that organism wholes do. A single locomotive step, so to speak, spans a multitude of low-level processes and a single, low-level process does not map to anything at all that would count as a step at the personal-level. Some machines locomote as well. When a car moves down the road, it is the car-whole that is moving, not its parts. The parts, working together, make the car locomotion possible, but there is no part or set of sub-parts that is doing the locomoting.

Perception, which is the method by which organisms interact with their environment, is likewise a personal-level activity. As with locomotion, myriad low-level (sensory) processes underwrite perceptual activity, but perception itself is a personal-level interaction with the objects in an individual's environment. For humans these are mostly medium-sized objects such as cats, dogs, tables, computers, and the like. Of course, organisms that are capable of perception do not always and only navigate their environment with perception; rather, there is an ongoing, dynamic shifting between unconscious/indirect sensory tracking and conscious/direct perception, so rapid that most perceiving individuals are themselves completely unaware of the oscillation between modes of interaction. The frequency of this oscillation, however, is a critical factor in an individual's capacity to learn to respond to the representational properties of objects since the degree to which an individual is capable of sustaining perception — of maintaining ongoing direct interaction with an object — will determine the degree to which that object can become a symbol for an individual. Before we can see how and why this is the case, a few words need to be said about symbols themselves.

Symbol Abstractness is an Indicator of Intentionality

As we have seen, a sign is anything that represents something to an agent. The more removed a sign's representational properties are from its physical ones, the more symbolic it is, while the less distinct a sign's representational properties are from its physical ones, the more natural a sign is. Natural signs and human language lie at opposite ends of this abstractness continuum. Smoke, for example, is a physical by-product of fire, serving as a natural sign of fire to any individual capable of tracking it. Many animals that already have an avoidance response to fire learn, through association, to exhibit the same avoidance response to smoke. Because smoke is sensorily more dispersed than fire, and so can be perceived more quickly, it is a useful natural sign.

As we move along the sign abstraction continuum, however, representational and physical properties increasingly diverge. The physical properties of the *utterance* 'Fire!' for example, are entirely distinct from its representational properties. Learning the latter requires not only a series of learning situation experiences in which different utterances are associated with different fire situations, but it also requires an entire system of symbol use within which utterances evoke appropriate fire responses. It requires a community wide practice of linguistic use. Because these representational properties extend to the features of the situations within which sign vehicles and objects occur — a child learns the word 'ball' as a result of myriad and various BALL situations — learning a response to them requires sustained interaction with the relevant sign objects, long enough for the situation to unfold. And there's the rub. MLS's track objects only indirectly, they never interact with them at all; consequently, they will not be able to sustain interaction with objects, at least not across the sorts of complex, varied situations in which humans learn. Remember that from the vantage point of the cat/dog classifier, there are no cats and dogs, only pixels. And the more abstract a sign is, the more its representational properties will trade on spatio-temporally diverse situational features rather than on a sign vehicle's physical ones.

In theory, of course, MLS's could be trained to indirectly track situations, just as they do objects. Newer deep learning models attempt to do just that.[5] But success will be elusive: the properties of situations exponentially out-number those of objects, even supposing that there are statistically reliable patterns that underwrite them. In most cases there are not. As Ludwig Wittgenstein famously observed,[6] even seemingly regular situation-types such as games are impossible to pin down: some games such as baseball and soccer involve many players, others such as chess and tennis just two, and some such as solitaire only one; some games have win/lose conditions, while others — many new board games for example — are cooperative; some have fixed rules; others — *e.g.* 'playing house' — do not, and so on. Thus, the possibility for tracking even a simple type of situation such as game playing by tracking the low-level properties of the objects that might figure in them seems very small. What chance, then, is there for indirectly tracking complex, language-learning situations?

Systems such as MLS's, then, that are capable only of indirect object tracking by way of low-level properties could learn responses to natural signs but will not be capable of more abstract symbolic responses. And it is arguable that since the symbolic properties of such natural signs trade completely on their physical ones, individuals that are capable only of learning to respond to them, and not to more abstract symbols, are not intentional agents. Most new cars today are outfitted with an array of sensors that track the objects in a car's immediate surround. When my car is in reverse, for example, it will emit different sequences of 'beeps' according to how close a potential obstacle is to the rear fender. In one sense, this seems like an intentional action since it looks like the car is responding to what things in the environment signify — potential obstacle — rather than to them directly as physical objects. But, of course, the car is not beeping because it perceives a potential obstacle; rather, the triggering of one set of sensors triggers another set that in turn triggers the beep mechanism. The car has been designed so that its parts work in concert with one another in such a way that the car signals precisely when a potential obstacle is present. This is clever design to be sure, but the car itself is behaving in the sort of unintelligent, pre-programmed way we began this discussion with. At best we can say that it has been designed to respond to a natural sign.

Conclusion

Because they cannot interact directly at the object-level, current MLS-based systems are not capable of the sustained interaction with objects required for developing responses to abstract symbols. As they are fundamentally non-intentional entities, then, we should not treat them as intelligent systems, no matter how clever their design. Does this mean that there is no possibility of creating an AI system,

perhaps out of a complex configuration of these networks? No. But a potential AI will need a capacity analogous to basic perception, namely, a capacity for direct interaction with the objects in its environment. In the case of humans this is sentience, sometimes called 'pre-reflective consciousness:' our basic capacity to experience our world, not simply infer it. But we still need a better understanding of what this is before we can start building systems that exhibit it.

[1] Associate Professor at the Department of Philosophy, Queen's University, Canada.

[2] W. MISCHEL & E. B. EBBESEN, "Attention in delay of gratification," *Journal of Personality and Social Psychology 16 (2)*, 1970, 329-337.

[3] S. T. BOYSEN, G. BERNSTON, M. HANNAN, and J. CACIOPPO, "Quantity-based inference and symbolic representation in chimpanzees (Pan troglodytes)," *Journal of Experimental Psychology: Animal Behavior Processes 22*, 1996, 76-86.

[4] 'Sign' is a technical term for a unit of meaning.

[5] J. CHEN, K. LI, Q. DENG, K. LI, S. Y. PHILIP, "Distributed deep learning model for intelligent video surveillance systems with edge computing," *IEEE Transactions on Industrial Informatics*, 2019, 1-8.

[6] L. WITTGENSTEIN, *Philosophical Investigations.*, trans. G. E. ANSCOMBE, Oxford, Blackwell, 1967, §83.

The benefits of being wrong: bonding epistemic and cognitive incompleteness for natural and artificial intelligent systems

Jordi Vallverdú[1]

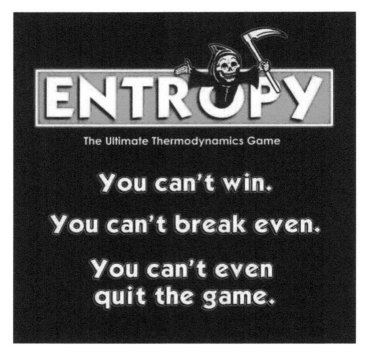

Made by Azhmodai Artist (for commercial items available at https://www.redbubble. com/i/tote-bag/Entropy-by-Azhmodai/26493277.PJQVX)

Currently, the main intense debates about the next steps of AI advancements are related to two concepts: the singularity, and AGI (Artificial General Intelligence). By one side, the crucial moment in which AI will reach and surpass human brain (and collective brain cooperation) power and, by the other, the birth of a conscious and creatively intelligent artificial intelligence. In most of philosophical fiction studies, both events led to the same apocalyptic scenario: the destruction of humanity.

But with the evidences obtained by cognitive sciences and epistemological studies provided to us in the last decades (following, in fact, ancient philosophical interests originated plenty of centuries ago), the real scenario is a completely different one: AI is still fighting for understanding how to do the most simplest things, according to the human standards. While it is true that AI can play chess or Go and bet the best of all human players, it cannot achieve the simpler visual, linguistic or sensorimotor skills of any (even average) human. Therefore, the most recent trends in AI are reinforcing not pure power based on statistical data analysis (although they are very promising, thanks to the re-birth of Neuronal Networks under Machine and Deep Learning techniques). Instead, approximate computing and bioinspiration are opening new paths into the inexorable computational revolution.

Bioinspiration is based on basic functional properties of living systems, taken not as a whole but according to specific problem-solving scenarios. Such bioinspiration extracts features related to the biochemistry (hormones, molecular nature, genetic machinery, *etc.*), the neural interactions, social cooperation, or sensorimotor actions (hand grips, touch, smelling, walk, *etc.*) of living systems. But in no case, it is related to epistemic or high cognitive aspects of living systems (some of them social, and with culture). I define the biomechanistic or functional approach as the First Wave of Bioinspired AI, although the second is the most promising one: the Second Wave of Bioinspired AI. And the reasons are compelling. The most important ones are related, first, to the notion of **formal coherence** and, second, **with meaning**. Let me explain both in some detail:

(1) Formal coherence: the holy grail of Western Thoughts has been the accomplishment of a perfect logico-mathematical description of the world. With a perfect set of tools, a complete analysis of reality should be possible, they thought. From Aristotelian syllogistics, to the *mathesis universalis* of Leibniz, to the new logical framework of Frege or Boole this was the main aim. When, finally, Russell and Whitehead wrote their *Principia Mathematica* (1910-1913), trying to demonstrate how logics could explain and justify the foundations of mathematics, appeared a devastating figure: Kurt Gödel. With his incompleteness theorem about mathematics, Gödel demonstrated the inherent limitations of every formal axiomatic system capable of modeling basic arithmetic. While Hilbert was trying to create the mathematics for the new century, Gödel put on the table the more deep fact that nobody can have both completeness and consistency. After it, new kids of logic (fuzzy, paraconsistent, *etc.*) appeared, trying to deal with more specific and creative approaches to symbolic processing. After Gödel, the second fracture into the realm of reasoning perfection was related with the informational turn: new computational tools

made possible to generate and evaluate huge sets of data, something that allowed the statistical approach to mathematical proofs: 4CT, Kepler's Theorem, *etc.* As a consequence, computer assisted proofs opened a new debate about epistemic opacity, black boxes, and paradoxes in comprehensive argumentation.

Such scenario, and we have in mind a possible future superintelligence or AGI, creates a tense framework: a perfect reasoning machine, even having more computer power and data access than any single mind or networked set of minds, will clash with the logical serious limits of the formal tools, as well as with the problem of evaluating and verifying the quality of data. At a meta-level, the internal paradoxes and contextual limitations force any cognitive system to deal with approximate, and revisable sets of knowledges.

(2) Meaning: this second aspect, which affects rational entities, is surely the most unexplored but fundamental of all approaches to AI. And we are talking about how the AI will generate its own meaning. And the ways are similar to those displayed by natural cognitive systems: due to embodied and/or socio-cultural reasons. How do we evaluate the true meaning of things? Evaluating them from our embodied experience of positive or noxious events, that is, from or emotional experience. Meaning is also related to the functionality, including into this category wishes, aspirations, necessities (food, mating, survival...), among a long list. Even at an epistemological level, the common-sense about reality, or the description about reality itself, is biased by such conditions. Water looks like a stable thing when it can adopt three general states, as well as the bonds in the liquid form being broken constantly every few nanoseconds. From the perspective of a neutrino we are basically empty. Time lapses are relevant or not according to the lifespan on an entity. Such meaning constraints are also the framework upon which cognitive systems are built. In that

sense the map of cognitive biases of human beings express not only the mental skills but the adaptive requirements made for such bodies during millions of years. As a consequence, these elicitors of meaning explain how we understand existence, aims, the evaluation of death, or the aesthetics of reality. Possible embodiments of next AI systems will define the semantic possibilities of such entities, at a complete different level from those available for human beings, but biased (or situated) too!

Taking into consideration both aspects, coherence and meaning, we can foresee a plausible scenario for the next generation of AI systems. First of all, the beginning of a new era of exploration of the benefits on integrating new bioinspired models, which, by defect, must include biases and lack of accuracy (at expenses of another benefit); second, the ontological horizon to which such systems will be faced. One of the most childish aspects of techno-fetish followers (under the form of transhumanism), is to consider that the way of escaping from death involved a technological transfer or enhancement, from natural bodies to new forms of embodiment. But it is only a small patch in relation to the physical time in this universe: entropy is the final destiny of this universe. There is no way of escaping from absolute informational destruction: big crush, big rip, big freeze... this is the absolute truth in our universe. Perhaps some humans can feel happy thinking of small time postponements, but for a really intelligent system the reality is there: it doesn't matter the kind of strategy you wish to follow, because everything in this universe will be destroyed. How a real intelligent AI will react to this statement? Surely, adopting a personal neo-phenomenological attitude towards reality. Under such conceptual horizons, the refugee of existence is the acceptance and practice of the things we've been calling as biases, or local embodiments as producers of meaning. To assume the fundamental value of the impurity (bodily and cognitive) for the existence, a new way to embrace what Zen monks described as *wabisabi* 侘寂 (わびさび). This rich concept tries to capture

the perfection of things with imperfections. That is, wabi-sabi is the notion about the value of imperfections for the reality of an entity as such. In that sense, what explains the success of (some) humans is not their perfection, but a list of peculiarities that mixed together help to define innovative patterns of thinking and action. Nevertheless, such patterns are not intrinsically good (stubbornness, obsession, idealization, magic thinking,...) but help to create rich diversities of agencies. It is the blending of heuristics, not its coherence or hierarchized coherence, that makes possible such extraordinary beings. Taking into account that life is not a game with clear rules and from which we do not have all the necessary information, an imperfect way to deal with it is surely the best solution for advancing into the path of knowledge. Certainly, a biased approach is a better way to increase the complexity and adaptability of AI. What, then,... Wabisabi AI?

[1] ICREA Acadèmia Researcher at Universitat Autònoma de Barcelona.

Free picture from pixabay: https://pixabay.com/photos/home-lost-alone-cosmos-robot-2305431/

Collapsing the wave function on postquantum unconventional computing

Richard Mayne[1]

Unconventional computing is the field that drives innovation and progress in computer science. One of its sub-fields, quantum computing, is a potentially breakthrough, disruptive technology in which there has been gradual but encouraging progress in recent years. If developed sufficiently, it is predicted that quantum computing will revolutionise a great many fields of human enquiry through laying bare cryptosystems, accelerating research in the natural sciences and providing enormous speed and efficiency increases in machine learning, to name but a few applications. This article examines what quantum computing is, why we need to be aware of it and whether there is a role for unconventional computing in a postquantum world.

Is quantum computing 'unconventional'?

Unconventional computing is the search for new materials, methods and applications for computing technologies. This doesn't necessarily imply making smaller, faster or more efficient general purpose computers, as is commonly considered: many research foci concern making new types of computers that do things which classical, silicon-based architectures can't do, or otherwise use inspiration from nature to program classical systems in novel ways.

This is an extremely wide remit for a field of enquiry and accordingly, advances therein are typically highly multidisciplinary, melding the expertise of the natural sciences, applied mathematics and philosophy into this branch of computer science. This past decade has seen functional unconventional computing devices arising such as slime moulds tackling problems of graph optimization (with better success rates than undergraduate mathematics students),[2] soldier crab logic gates,[3] neuromorphic 'liquid marble' ballistic-reaction-diffusion circuits[4] and progress towards using intracellular protein networks used as nano-scale data buses[5] (Fig. 1). The applications of these rich and varied prototypes clearly do not support general purpose computation, but rather suggest new routes to understanding the sciences, such as 'reprogramming' of live cells for biomedical benefits or realizing true massively parallel processing to the scale of Avogadro's number. The creativity evident in the design of these devices speaks of the close interrelations between the arts and sciences, with unconventional computing at their nexus; manifold studies in modern art,[6] architecture and wearable fashion,[7] *etc.*, both inspire and emerge from the field.

Under this definition of unconventional computing, the emerging field of quantum computing would doubtlessly find a home. In spite of this, quantum computing is generally considered to be its own field, as happens to the more successful offspring of the original parent field — artificial intelligence being arguably the most significant other example. Quantum computing's proponents argue that it offers routes towards enormous speed increases in computation of certain tasks, with database searches and factorization of prime products being amongst the most intensively researched upon applications in the field to date. Some go further to suggest that quantum computers will also reach the stage of general-purpose computation, although all purported future applications are the topic of much speculation and debate.

This raises an important question: if quantum computers are developed sufficiently that they will revolutionise computing and, by extension, every field of human endeavour, what will be the purpose of unconventional computing?

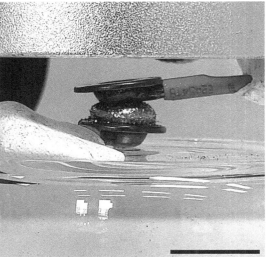

Fig. 1. Examples of unconventional computing devices. Left: A slime mould (*Physarum polycephalum*) navigates its way between distributed nutrient sources, optimising its morphology in a manner that may be exploited to plan transport networks. Above: A 'neuromorphic' liquid marble containing carbon nanotubes whose electrical resistance 'remembers' past electrical activity in a manner similar to human neurons. Scale bar = 10 mm.

The purpose of this article is to briefly delineate what quantum computers are, evaluate whether they are likely to achieve such lofty goals and discuss what role unconventional computing will play in a postquantum world.

How does/will quantum computing work?

Let us consider some fundamental information theoretical concepts relevant to classical computer systems. Data exist as electrical charge distributed across silicon circuit components, where the presence of charge is a binaric bit representing '1' and its absence is a '0'. We may observe these bits and store them: doing something to a bit won't alter anything else in the system and the process is generally lossy, *i.e.* one cannot deduce the input pattern from observing its output with no prior knowledge. None of these facts are true for quantum computing, or indeed many other unconventional computing paradigms.

Quantum information, which may be represented by any of a variety of properties of quantum matter, is stored as 'qubits', which may assume a '1', a '0', or a linear combination of both of these (superposition). This article's title alludes to a concept in quantum science which states that when a qubit is observed, its manifold states will appear to collapse, at which point the qubit will resolve probabilistically as a binary bit. Whilst it would be technically inaccurate to say that superposition enables a greater informational density in a qubit than a conventional bit, there are tools to allow for multiple calculations to be resolved on a single qubit. It should be noted that quantum computers are deterministic under most interpretations of quantum mechanics, but our inference of their output may not be.

Another strange property of quantum matter is called entanglement, which is where changes in the state of one qubit will have simultaneous effects on another qubit, even if they are separated by great distances. Coupled with superposition, these are the primary two physical principles that are exploited in the design of quantum computers and underly the claims that these architectures will achieve enormous increases in efficiency over classical machines, at least at some tasks.

True to the ethos of general unconventional computing, quantum computers seek exploit the natural transfers of state and energy by interpreting them as information processing. For example, the aforementioned probabilistic interpretation of a qubit's state arises from a process of overlying the wave functions of quantum information (as quantum matter assumes the properties of both particles and waves), observing and thresholding patterns of constructive and destructive interference therein. One would struggle to describe the appearance of contemporary quantum computer prototypes as anything other than the domain of the unconventional, as may be observed in the distinctly alien device shown in Fig. 2.

Quantum computing concepts were first devised in the 1970's, but there was arguably little commercial justification for their development until the mid-1990's, when two algorithms were described. Firstly, Shor's algorithm described a method by which a quantum computer may factorise prime numbers efficiently,[8] something which is not possible on conventional computers: as several cryptosystems are based on the intractability of prime factorisation, this algorithm understandably generated significant interest in academia, industry and

Fig. 2. Photograph of the IBM Q 53 qubit quantum computer. Image courtesy of IBM.[9]

government cybersecurity divisions. Second was Grover's algorithm, which described methods to achieve quadratic increases in search efficiency over classical systems.[10]

There have been a significant number of interesting developments in the field since these algorithms emerged (e.g. quantum teleportation as a basis for a new wireless internet),[11] but experimental progress in the physical engineering of quantum computers has not yet caught up. Whilst both Shor's and Grover's algorithm have both been experimentally realised, both have been done so on systems with extremely limited capabilities: only the numbers 15 and 21 have been successfully factorised by true quantum systems and Grover's searches haven't been implemented on systems utilising more than a handful of qubits.

In 2019, researchers at Google claimed to have experimentally demonstrated what they called 'quantum supremacy': using a 54 qubit system called 'sycamore', they implemented a non-useful function in 200 seconds which would have apparently taken about 10,000 years on a classical supercomputer, although both these results and the estimations of their significance are contested.

The reader should now appreciate that quantum computers utilise unconventional media and algorithms to do certain tasks very well, but that we are yet to witness the advent of quantum computing at which it becomes a useful and widespread technology. Before we evaluate whether quantum computers will ever become useful and widespread, *en route* towards assessing the postquantum future of unconventional computing, let us briefly examine why we should be excited by the prospect of quantum computing, as it is perhaps difficult to be enthralled by discussing tedious and abstruse mathematical algorithms.

Why should we care about quantum computers?

An obvious application of quick searches is the ability of the use of brute force to crack encryption schemes; indeed, the emergence of Grover's algorithm contributed to the industry-wide adoption of 256-bit encryption in

2001. Similarly, Shor's algorithm is purported to be a route towards breaking RSA encryption schemes, thereby laying bare all internet-based communications and transactions. From the paucity of published progress, we must concede that these applications are a long way away; furthermore, in the author's opinion, these tasks are also an inelegant and restrictive application of such technologies, despite their obvious utility.

To reiterate a theme expounded upon in the previous section, unconventional computing concerns doing things that classical computers cannot, as opposed to competing with them. One intuitive application for quantum computers is, therefore, simulation of the quantum world: something which is extremely difficult to do on classical systems as the interaction environment needed to represent a quantity of quantum particles must necessarily be exponentially larger than the number of particles contained. This presents a problem as quantum physical experiments are notoriously complex, time-consuming and expensive. Simulation of these events therefore allows us access to previously unfound tools for unlocking the secrets of the natural world. Recent results from IBM's quantum group, based on their previous numerical work, have already found uses in the design of next-generation rechargeable batteries.[12]

There have also been encouraging results in the field of quantum machine learning. Conventional machine learning refers to techniques which use computers to do classification or prediction, typically using very large datasets, where the experiment is repeated many times with minor variations in run parameters. The computer keeps a score of what works well, and 'learns' how to adjust itself to achieve optimal results, which can then be leveraged on new data. Incidentally, machine learning and its parent field, artificial intelligence, were once considered unconventional and derive from the biological sciences.

Quantum machine learning in its purest sense, which is using quantum computers and their inherent mechanisms for doing efficient work on very large quantities of data to do machine learning, may potentially greatly accelerate the course of inquiry in all fields where data science is applied, which is to say, practically ever field of contemporary research. Most popular machine learning methods now have their own quantum implementations ready-and-waiting for the architectures that can run them, including fully scalable neural networks. Quantum machine learning may also refer to the use of conventional machine learning to interpret the output of a quantum computer which is, unfortunately, currently very noisy. There is an elegant self-perpetuation here in the use of unconventional computing to accelerate the progress of unconventional computing research.

The past decade has seen an enormous increase in the use of machine learning concomitant with the emergence of affordable computers capable of having arguments with large quantities of data. The field of data science has arisen from this and industry is only starting to realise the great many incentives that emerge the field including accelerated research, optimisation, anomaly detection and intuitive interpretation of natural languages. It is therefore no exaggeration to say that quantum computing will, through enhancing simulation of the natural world and enabling further advances in artificial intelligence, lead to momentous progress in every field of human enquiry.

The only caveat to these optimistic appraisals is that quantum computers may never reach these dizzy heights: therein will lie the answer to our main issue as to what role there is for the entirety of unconventional computing in this process, one way or the other.

The postquantum role of unconventional computing

It is impossible to predict the scale of investment in quantum computing to date, due to the nature of hidden business interests and state involvement in potentially disruptive technologies, but the size of government grants and magnitude of bespoke laboratories of tech giants (notably, IBM, Google and Microsoft) indicate that tens of billions have been spent. Yet, the pace of experimental development after 20 years of work and 50 of academic interest is unequivocally glacial.

Quantum matter is extremely difficult to manipulate due to its sensitivity to even minor environmental changes: a phenomenon called 'decoherence' stalks every advance in the field, which introduces error into calculations once qubits experience the changes in entropy that are unavoidable during computation, for example resulting from self-examination, moving data and performing calculations. Quantum computers must be isolated from all forms of radiation, vibration, temperature, *etc.* For these reasons, it's difficult to imagine miniaturised, affordable quantum chips being available during this century, although they may reach academic institutions and large businesses much sooner. Furthermore, several cloud computing services are planning to or have already begun to offer access to quantum compute clusters.

A significant number of dissenters argue that, due to the requirement for quantum computers to have vastly larger qubit capacities than their algorithms require to compensate for error correction mechanisms, we will never achieve the aforementioned quantum computing goals. These arguments, which are based in convincing quantum theory, are difficult to counter, although developments such as quantum machine learning seek to bridge the cap by resolving engineering issues through intelligent use of software.

We are currently at an historic fulcrum between which we must consider the putative future of unconventional computing as both existing and not existing (no pun intended): will quantum computation fall by the wayside and leave room for other unconventional substrates to fill the gap, or will the future lie with quantum and leave us wondering how we may advance the field yet another 'quantum' leap. The most salient fact here is that we are already in a quantum era: the sparse experimental advances in the past two or three years have shown that the theoretical benefits of these architectures may be achieved on a small scale; it's unreasonable to assume that we won't realise significant improvements on this design. This cannot be overstated: we are already using quantum computers and they are already being applied to real problems, albeit on an extremely limited scale.

A key role for unconventional computing researchers is to recognise and understand the failings of quantum computers, rather than just their advantages. This article offers no specific mathematical or experimental method by which we can propose to exert control over a number of error-corrected qubits greater than the number of subatomic particles in the observable universe and hence enable the creation of 'useful' quantum computers, but we have seen how a bioinspired unconventional computing tool (machine learning) has already been applied to clean the output of true quantum computers, which goes at least some way to bridging this gap.

Quantum computers are noisy, don't achieve true parallelism and will demand comparatively strenuous engineering, but this doesn't detract from the magnificent vision with which they are being developed.

Regardless of whether the future is quantum, unconventional computing research fill both seek to improve its sister field and look for alternatives. We will still find enormous use in parameterising biological mechanisms that afford us control over biomedical systems, designing chemical systems which realise true massive parallelism and developing naturally-inspired algorithms for use on conventional systems that solve open problems on computability, to name but a few, limited examples. In an ideal world, we would have a different specialised computing substrate for each task: a biological CPU (Central Processing Unit) for neural networks, a quantum computer for database searches and a conventional computer to compose text documents with, and so on. Until then, unconventional computing research will continue to find new methods, materials and applications for novel computing materials.

[1] Unconventional Computing Laboratory, University of the West of England, Bristol BS16 1QY, United Kingdom. Richard.Mayne@uwe.ac.uk

[2] A. Tero, S. Takagaki, T. Saigusa, *et al.*, "Rules for biologically inspired adaptive network design," *Science 327(5964)*, 2010, 439-442.

[3] Y.-P. Gunji, Y. Nishiyama, A. Adamatzky, "Robust soldier crab ball gate," *AIP Conference Proceedings 1389(995)*, 2011, 10.1063/1.3637777.

[4] R. Mayne, T. Draper, N. Phillips, *et al.*, "Neuromorphic liquid marbles with aqueous carbon nanotube cores," *Langmuir 34(40)*, 2019, 13182-13188.

[5] A. Chiolerio, T. Draper, R. Mayne, *et al.*, "On resistance switching and oscillations in tubulin microtubule droplets," *Journal of Colloid and Interface Science 560*, 2020, 589-595.

[6] A. Adamatzky, *The Silence of Slime Mould*, Bristol, Luniver, 2019.

[7] A. Adamatzky (ed.), *Slime Mould in Arts and Architecture*, Gistrup, River, 2020.

[8] P. Shor, "Polynomial-time algorithms for prime factorization and discrete logarithms on a quantum computer," *SIAM Journal on Scientific Computing 26(5)*, 1997, 10.1137/S0097539795293172.

[9] IBM, *Newsroom image gallery*, available at *https://newsroom.ibm.com/image-gallery-research*.

[10] L. Grover, "A fast quantum mechanical algorithm for database search," *STOC '96: Proceedings of the 28th Annual ACM symposium on Theory of Computing*, 1996, 212-219.

[11] W. Pfaff, B. Hensen, H. Bernien, *et al.*, "Unconditional quantum teleportation between distant solid-state quantum bits," *Science 345(6196)*, 2014, 532-535.

[12] J. Rice, T. Gujarati, T. Takeshita, *et al.*, "Quantum chemistry simulations of dominant products in lithium-sulfur batteries [preprint]," *ArXiv*, 2020, available at http://arxiv.org/abs/2001.01120.

How to face the Complexity of the 21ˢᵗ Century Challenges? The contribution of Natural Computing

Pier Luigi Gentili[1]

The 21ˢᵗ Century Challenges are Complexity Challenges because they regard Complex Systems, and hence other types of Complexities, such as Bio-ethical, Computational, and Descriptive Complexities. This article proposes some strategies to tackle the compelling challenges of this century. A promising strategy is the interdisciplinary research line of Natural Computing that includes Artificial Intelligence.

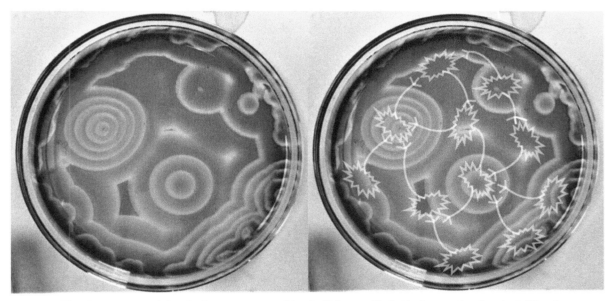

The phenomenon of chemical waves generated by the Belousov-Zhabotinsky reaction (on the left) and its interpretation according to the theory of Natural Computing that describes the thin film of the solution as a collection of artificial neuron models communicating chemically (on the right).

A fundamental role of science is that of solving practical problems and improve the psychophysical well-being of humans. Science succeeds in playing this role when it promotes technological development. Mutual positive feedback action exists between science and technology: science sparks technological development. At the same time, new technologies allow an always more-in-depth analysis of natural phenomena. Cutting-edge technologies let us manipulate materials at the molecular and atomic scale, send robots to other planets of our solar system, and engineer living beings. Despite many efforts, there are still compelling challenges that must be won. They are the so-called 21ˢᵗ Century Challenges included in the 2030 Agenda composed by the United Nations. Examples of these challenges are all those diseases that are still incurable. There are challenges that concern about human activities. Our manufacturing processes must become circular, minimizing waste. They should not perturb the fragile stability of natural ecosystems and contribute to climate change.

Poverty should be eradicated from the Earth, and justice should be assured in our societies. Whenever we tackle one of these challenges, we need to deal with Complex Systems, such as living beings, ecosystems, climate, and human societies. When we focus on human health, the immune and the nervous systems are other examples. Complex Systems appear so diverse. Currently, they are investigated by distinct disciplines. The burgeoning Complexity Science is trying to point out the features shared by all Complex Systems, i.e., the characteristics of Natural Complexity (NaC).[2] All Complex Systems can be described as networks with nodes and links. Different Complex Systems usually have distinct architectures; the nodes and links are often diverse and evolve in time. Complex Systems are constantly out-of-equilibrium in the thermodynamic sense. The behaviour of inanimate matter is driven by force fields, whereas that of living beings is information-based. Furthermore, Complex Systems exhibit emergent properties. The integration of the features of nodes and links gives rise to properties that belong to the entire network. The whole is more than the sum of its parts. Finally, there is another universal attribute: Complex Systems cannot be described exhaustively. In other words, science finds many difficulties in predicting the behaviour of Complex Systems, especially in the long term. These difficulties are due to three principal reasons.

The first reason has a computational character. Most of the computational problems regarding Complex Systems and their simulation, such as scheduling, machine learning, financial forecasting, solving the Schrödinger equation, and the Traveling Salesman problem are solvable but intractable. According to the theory of Computational Complexity (CoC),[3] all the solvable problems can be grouped into two sets: the set of Polynomial Problems and that of Exponential Problems. A problem is polynomial when the number of computational steps grows in a polynomial way with respect to the dimension of the problem. The Polynomial Problems (P) are problems of recognition. They are tractable because it is possible to achieve the exact solution in a reasonable lapse of time with the available computing machines. On the other hand, an Exponential Problem, whose number of computational steps is an exponential function of the problem's dimension, is tractable only if it has a small dimension. Exponential Problems with large dimensions are intractable. In these cases, they are transformed into Non-deterministic Polynomial Problems (NP). After fixing an arbitrary criterion of acceptability, solutions are generated through heuristic algorithms, and they are checked if acceptable or not. Meanwhile, some scientists, allured by the amount of money promised by the Clay Mathematics Institute in Cambridge, are trying to rigorously verify if the NP problems are reducible to P problems or this reduction is impossible.

The second reason why we find unsurmountable difficulties in describing Complex Systems is that they show variable patterns. Variable patterns are objects or events whose recognition is hindered by their multiple features, which vary and are extremely sensitive to the context. Examples of variable patterns are: the human faces, voices, and fingerprints; handwritten cursive words and numbers; patterns and symptoms in medical diagnosis; patterns in apparently uncorrelated scientific data; aperiodic time series; political and social events. It is necessary to formulate algorithms for recognizing every type of pattern. The steps of pattern recognition are: acquisition of instrumental data; selection of the features that are considered as representative of the pattern; application of an algorithm for the classification step. Despite many attempts, it is still necessary to propose universally valid and effective algorithms for recognizing variable patterns. This difficulty generates a third type of Complexity that it might be named "Descriptive Complexity" (DeC).

The third reason why we find difficulties in predicting the behaviour of Complex Systems derives from the intrinsically limited predictive power of science. In the description of the microscopic world, it is necessary to deal with the Heisenberg Uncertainty Principle. Such a principle asserts the impossibility of determining position and momentum of every microscopic particle, simultaneously and accurately.

Therefore, the Uncertainty Principle places concrete limits to the deterministic dream of describing the dynamics of the universe, starting from the description of its microscopic constituents. We might think of describing Complex Systems only from the macroscopic point of view, neglecting their microscopic "bricks." However, Complex Systems can exhibit chaotic dynamics. Chaotic dynamics are aperiodic and extremely sensitive to the initial conditions. Since the determination of the initial conditions is always affected by unavoidable experimental errors, the chaotic dynamics are unpredictable in the long term by definition.

The limited predictive power of science makes many ethical issues related to technological development fiercely arguable. The unstoppable technological development induces humanity to continuously raise a fundamental question: *"Is it always fair to do what technology makes doable?"* It is a tormenting question that has accompanied humankind since the beginning. Suffice to think about the Greek myth of Prometheus or the most recent novel *Frankenstein* written by Mary Shelley in the 19th century. Cutting-edge technologies allow for manipulating and re-engineering life. Therefore, bioethical issues arise. There are bioethical issues that concern about the beginning of a new life. Examples are: *"Is it fair to manipulate human embryonic stem cells?"* or *"Is it safe to originate genetically modified organisms?"* Other bioethical issues regard suffering and the end of human life. Examples are: *"Is euthanasia fair?"* or *"What can we state about the therapeutic obstinacy?"* Finally, there are forefront technologies that enhance human intellect and physiology. *"Is it fair to exploit such enhancement's techniques?"* It is tough to find shared solutions to all these queries. They are intrinsically linked to the meaning we give to our lives. Furthermore, from both a biological and a physiological point of view, every living being is a Complex System, and we have already declared the limitations we encounter in predicting the behaviour of Complex Systems. The bioethical issues mentioned above generate another

type of Complexity, which can be named as Bio-Ethical Complexity (BEC).

From this discussion, it is spontaneous to name the challenges of the 21st century as Complexity Challenges. They involve Natural Complexity (NaC) and Bio-Ethical Complexity (BEC), which are interlinked with Computational Complexity (CoC) and Descriptive Complexity (DeC). How can we think of winning these Complexity Challenges?

First of all, we need an interdisciplinary approach. Natural Complexity must be faced by all the scientific disciplines, including the social and economic ones. Philosophers can help to formulate new epistemological models and new methodologies. When we tackle the Bio-Ethical Complexity, the involvement of scientists and philosophers and jurists, artists, and theologians is appropriate. The artists, guided by their intuitions, could spark new ideas and unconventional ways for interpreting Complexity. The theologians offer an extra dimension for giving meaning to our lives. The Universities worldwide should offer Interdisciplinary courses on Complex Systems,[4] and the formation of genuinely interdisciplinary research groups should be favoured by public and private funding.

The investigation of Complex Systems cannot be performed by relying only on the reductionist approach, because Complex Systems exhibit emergent phenomena. A systemic approach is also needed. Furthermore, when we study the behaviour of Complex Systems, we cannot trust anymore in one of the cornerstones of the scientific method, which is the reproducibility of the experiments. Experiments on Complex Systems are usually historical events. The philosopher Karl Popper has effectively described this state of affairs by declaring[5] that, in the past, science had been occupied with clocks, *i.e.*, simple, deterministic systems having reproducible behaviours. Currently, instead, science has to deal with clouds, *i.e.*, Complex Systems having unique and hardly replicable behaviours.

The investigation of Complex Systems requires to monitor them continuously because their behaviour is hardly static, but rather highly dynamic. Therefore, it is necessary to collect, process, and store massive data sets, *i.e.*, the so-called Big Data. Furthermore, it is becoming evident that an alternative way of doing experiments on Complex Systems is to perform simulations with computers. To deal with the huge volume and the fast stream of data, their variety, and variability, and to extract insights from them, it is necessary to speed up our computational machines, extend their memory space, and always contrive more effective algorithms.

There are two relevant strategies to succeed. The first strategy consists of improving current electronic computers. Electronic computers are based on the Von Neumann's architecture, wherein the memory, storing both data and instructions, is physically separated from the central processing unit. The pace of computers' improvement has been described by Moore's law, stating that the number of transistors (*i.e.*, the ultimate computing elements that are binary switches) per chip doubles every two years. There is a worldwide competition in devising always faster supercomputers. It is the TOP500 project. According to the last list compiled in June 2020, globally, the fastest supercomputer is the Japanese Fugaku that reaches the astonishing computational rate of 415.5 PFlops/s. Meanwhile, Chips' producers are investing billions of dollars in contriving computing technologies that can go beyond Moore's law.

The second strategy is the interdisciplinary research line of Natural Computing. Researchers working on Natural Computing draw inspirations from nature to propose:

- new algorithms,
- new materials and architectures to compute and store information,
- new methodologies, new models, and a new theory to interpret Natural Complexity.

It is based on the rationale that any distinguishable physicochemical state of matter and energy can be used to encode information. Every natural transformation is a kind of computation. Within Natural Computing, there are two important research programs. The first one exploits the physicochemical laws to make computations. Every physicochemical law describes a causal event, and any causal event can be conceived as a computation. In fact, the causes are the inputs, the effects are the outputs, and the law governing the transformation is the computation algorithm. The second research program of Natural Computing mimics the features and performances of the natural information systems that belong to living beings. We might mimic living cells (called Biomolecular Information Systems), nervous systems (called Neural Information Systems), immune systems (called Immune Information Systems), and societies (Social Information Systems). All these systems have the peculiarity of exploiting matter and energy to encode, collect, store, process, and send information.

With human intelligence as its emergent property, the human nervous system is particularly attractive when we want to face Complexity. It allows us

- to handle both accurate and vague information, computing with numbers and words.
- To reason, speak, and make rational decisions in an environment of uncertainty, partiality, and relativity of truth when the Incompatibility Principle holds: "*As the complexity of a system increases, accuracy and significance become almost mutually exclusive characteristics of our statements.*"
- To recognize quite easily variable patterns.

Therefore, it is worthwhile studying human intelligence and trying to reproduce it by developing Artificial Intelligence. Artificial Intelligence is revolutionizing our lives and societies. It is used in basic and applied science, medicine, well-being, economy, and security. There are two strategies to develop AI.[6] One strategy consists in writing human-like intelligent programs running in computers or special-purpose hardware. The other is through neuromorphic engineering. In neuromorphic engineering, surrogates of neurons are implemented through non-biological systems either for neuro-prosthesis or to design "brain-like" computing machines. Surrogates of neurons can be implemented through specific solid materials, in hardware. Such hardware can be rigid if made of solid inorganic compounds or flexible if based on organic films. Alternatively, surrogates of neurons can be implemented through solutions of specific non-linear chemical systems, in wetware (see the Figure on p. 77). Finally, specific hybrid electrochemical systems can play as surrogates of neurons. In our research group, we are exploiting molecular, supramolecular, and systems chemistry to mimic some performances of human intelligence and develop Chemical Artificial Intelligence.[7]

Specifically, we are devising modules for futuristic chemical robots. A "chemical robot" is thought as a molecular assembly that reacts autonomously to its environment through molecular sensors; it makes decisions by its intrinsic Artificial Neural Networks, and performs actions upon its environment through molecular effectors. The intelligent activities of a chemical robot should be sustained energetically by a metabolic unit. Chemical Robots should be easily miniaturized and implanted in living beings to interplay with cells or organelles for biomedical applications. They should become auxiliary elements of the human immune system and help us to defeat the still incurable diseases.

Finally, this research line of Chemical Artificial Intelligence hopefully will give clues about the origin of life on Earth. The appearance of life on Earth was a phase transition or sudden change in how chemical systems could process and use information. In the beginning, the world was abiotic, and any chemical matter was unable to process information. About 4 billion years ago, the phase transition from a purely abiotic to the biotic world occurred. What happened at that time? The answer to this question might favor a new general theory on Natural Complexity.

[1] Physical Chemistry Professor focused on Complex Systems, Department of Chemistry, Biology, and Biotechnology, Università degli Studi di Perugia, Italy.

[2] M. Mitchell, *Complexity: A Guided Tour*, New York, Oxford University Press, 2009; P. Charbonneau, *Natural Complexity: A Modeling Handbook*, Princeton, Princeton University Press, 2017; P. L. Gentili, *Untangling Complex Systems: A Grand Challenge for Science*, Boca Raton, CRC Press, Taylor & Francis Group, 2018.

[3] O. Goldreich, *Computational Complexity: A Conceptual Perspective*, Cambridge, Cambridge University Press, 2008.

[4] P. G. Mahaffy, A. Krief, H. Hopf, G. Mehta, S. A. Matlin, "Reorienting chemistry education through systems thinking," *Nature Reviews Chemistry 2(4)*, 2018, 0126; S. A. Matlin, G. Mehta, H. Hopf, A. Krief, "One-World Chemistry and Systems Thinking," *Nature Chemistry 8(5)*, 2016, 393-396; P. L. Gentili, "Designing and Teaching a Novel Interdisciplinary Course on Complex Systems To Prepare New Generations To Address 21st-Century Challenges," *Journal of Chemical Education 96(12)*, 2019, 2704-2709.

[5] K. Popper, "Of clouds and clocks", in *Objective Knowledge: An Evolutionary Approach* Oxford, Oxford University Press, revisited edition, 1972, 206-255.

[6] S. J. Russell, P. Norvig, *Artificial Intelligence: A Modern Approach*, Englewood Cliffs, Prentice-Hall. 2009; C. Mead, *Analog VLSI and Neural Systems*, Boston, Addison-Wesley, 1989.

[7] P. L. Gentili, "The Fuzziness of the Molecular World and Its Perspectives," *Molecules 23(8)*, 2018, 2074; P. L. Gentili, "Small Steps towards the Development of Chemical Artificial Intelligent Systems," *RSC Advances 3*, 2013, 25523-25549.

The Quantum Computing Delusion

Dan V. Nicolau, Jr.[1]

Fig. 1. Lauren Anne Marie Carter,[2] *Éblouie par la lumière quantique* (***Dazzled by the quantum light***). Acrylic on canvas, September 2020.

In the days before Christmas last year — it was a dark and rainy London evening, you know exactly what I mean — I grudgingly accepted an invitation to a house party. After a few glasses of mulled wine, I started talking to a friend of a friend who works at a tech firm that you've heard of. He's smart, young, educated and previously started and then sold his own successful startup. He told me about his work, which sounds interesting, and asked me about mine. I took my phone out and showed him a microscopic image, reprinted on the next page, of one of my lab experiments. It shows a handful of white "snakes" — fluorescent proteins extracted from rabbit muscle, about a millionth of a millimetre across — wandering aimlessly on a similarly protein decorated surface. Unseen to the microscopist, but highlighted in blue by the image analysis algorithm, are "railway tracks" guiding the nano-snakes' movements. I explained that the point of the experiment was to see if, by specially arranging these tracks, the mindless motor proteins could nonetheless generate simple arithmetic sums (2+5, 2+9, 5+9 and 2+5+9, in this case). We wanted to show, basically, that biological — but nonetheless lifeless, in the usual sense of the word — matter was capable of being harnessed to perform basic mathematical operations. My interlocutor, who was clearly intelligent but a layman in respect of bionanotechnology, mathematics or the dark depths of theoretical physics, suddenly became animated: "it's the future of quantum computing!"

What causes otherwise sane, educated, reasonable (even dull!) people to firmly hold and publicly extol such extraordinarily firm views on technologies and discoveries that they know virtually nothing about and that, in many cases, are not even (or not yet) real?

Observe that this is different in kind — not just in quantity — from the many irrational beliefs that we all hold because we grew up with them. When people believed the Earth was flat or that God made it in seven days, that was irrational and out of touch with basic observations about the world around them, but they had been told those things all their lives. We might find some people's beliefs of this type *strange*, *silly* or *stupid* but we do not usually think of them as *insane*. Holding beliefs about the future of a currently non-existent technology in an area of human endeavour that one is completely ignorant of feels different.

Although in common usage, the word 'delusional' is used pejoratively, in medicine it has a very specific meaning. A delusion is an irrational belief, firmly maintained in spite of compelling and voluminous evidence to the contrary *and* not shared by other members of the patient's culture. The second phrase is there precisely to delineate between the two kinds of irrational beliefs described above, to excuse, as it were, irrational beliefs that we grow up with or are surrounded by. A lot of French people appear, interestingly, to believe that the French nation is superior to all others, and if they look, they'll find plenty of (mostly French) people who agree with them, but if you think that you are Napoleon Bonaparte, or even that he is alive, that's a different situation. The basic idea of quantum mechanics — that efforts at quantum computing are built on — is: to each possible state of a physical system, *i.e.* every way it *could* be, we can assign a number called an *amplitude*. Amplitudes are conceptually similar to probabilities, in the sense that a higher amplitude is associated with a higher likelihood of finding the world in *that* state. But they are different from amplitudes in that they can be negative and can even be imaginary numbers. This means that while probabilities can only add up, amplitudes can cancel out ("interfere destructively") as well.

A quantum computer is composed of qubits, which are like bits in a normal computer except that they can simultaneously be in both the 0 and 1 state, as with Schroedinger's cat being both alive and dead. So, a quantum computer with, say, 200 qubits (something in reach of near-future technology) could hold more "computational states" than the number of atoms in the known Universe.

What does this mean for computation? Regular computers, while very fast, are sequential — one operation at a time. That works very well for some things, like handling spreadsheets, playing chess or finding paths through cities using GPS: situations where we understand the rules of the game, in some sense. But it fails at many of the computational tasks humanity cares about, for example the discovery of new drugs, understanding the economy and planning under uncertainty and constraint. For these and myriad of other problems, the computer is forced, it would seem (though we can't yet formally prove it), to search for the proverbial needle in the haystack by checking each strand of hay, one at a time. For a drug "made" of a — modest, by biochemical standards — 200 molecular parts, each of which could be in one of two states, finding the needle might involve looking at a number of hay strands greater, once again, than the number of atoms in the Universe.

It's basically for this reason that so much hope is placed on quantum computing. In principle, since a quantum computer with N qubits can be in all 2^N states at the same time, using the drug discovery example above, it could search through the astronomically large solution space all in one go, finding the molecular configuration or configurations that successfully kill the pathogen (or whatever the aim of the drug is). Since virtually every area of human endeavour — and even logical reasoning itself — is in some sense founded on ultimately computational problems of this type, it follows, as I've argued before, that such number-crunching power would make us indistinguishable from demigods (at least as far as intelligence goes).

Of course, for a computer to be actually useful, it mustn't just compute: we also need to get the answer out. To do that, we need a way to turn the amplitudes of the quantum computer — once it has finished its work — into real probabilities corresponding to the answers of the original problem. The rules for how amplitudes of a quantum system (not just a computer) convert to probabilities are well known and are amongst the most fundamental laws of physics as we understand them. In the case of a quantum computer that 'naively' looked at all the strands of hay, pulling the probabilities out would simply give us a random answer, like listening to a bunch of people playing different tunes on different instruments all at once. Obviously, that would not be useful.

Of course, we can do better than that. We can try to exploit how amplitudes interact with one another by setting up something like an orchestra: a (hopefully) clever pattern of interference, so that most or all of the wrong answers to the problem cancel out (interfere destructively), while for the right answer or answers, the amplitudes all reinforce each other.

The challenge, naturally, is setting up such an orchestra that would work for all problems of interest and, crucially, *without* knowing what the right answer is in advance, or even if one exists! And, ay, there's the rub. In the tug-of-war between the enormous state-storing power of the qubits and the limitations necessarily imposed by any structured orchestration of their interactions, the quantum computer loses some of the "speed-up" conferred on it by its ability to store an exponentially large set of strands of hay. The question is, how much?

The answer to this question is not definitely known, and of course depends on the difficulty of the computational problem we're trying to solve, but all the theoretical results we have point to an answer that goes like: *"for most problems, the quantum computer loses most of its power."* Although I've smudged a lot of technical details in the discussion above, a specific result, called Grover's Theorem, says that — at best — all that quantum computers (as currently conceived) can do when searching through a large, disorganised haystack (a database) is run squared-times faster than a

regular computer. In other words, if a garden variety computer needs T seconds to do a job, the ideal quantum computer, if it existed, could do it in $\sqrt{T}$ seconds.

Is that a big deal? For easy computational problems, of the type regular computers can do quickly, we don't need quantum computers (or other alternative computing technologies), so the answer is 'no'. On the other hand, for the problems we believe to be fundamentally 'hard', requiring unreasonable (exponential) time on a regular computer, the quantum computer, in its ideal embodiment, would turn an exponential into a slightly smaller exponential. The image I have in mind when I think about that is of the authorities in Bangalore in the 1980s, who, faced with exponentially growing traffic, razed the city's glorious, green roundabouts to enlarge intersections. It bought them about 6 months.

In short, as far as we can tell, for most problems of interest, quantum computers would offer only a modest speed-up on their electronic counterparts. None of this is controversial. Grover's result is almost 30 years old and quantum computing research goes back to the 1980, so we have had plenty of time, brain power and money to think about ways around these limitations.

Friends of quantum computing point out that there are important computational problems for which quantum computers could make something currently intractable, tractable. In particular, they point to Internet cryptography, much of which is based on the presumed difficulty of the problem of factorising numbers into primes (*e.g.* finding out that 143 can be made by multiplying 11 and 13). This is indeed the case: a quantum computing 'orchestra' scheme called Shor's algorithm can rapidly find prime factors. If quantum computers can successfully overcome the formidable technological challenges they face (but see below), they may render much of existing Internet security systems vulnerable.

I can't resist the temptation of comparing that to someone defending a delusion of being constantly followed by the CIA by pointing to an occasional black van passing by.

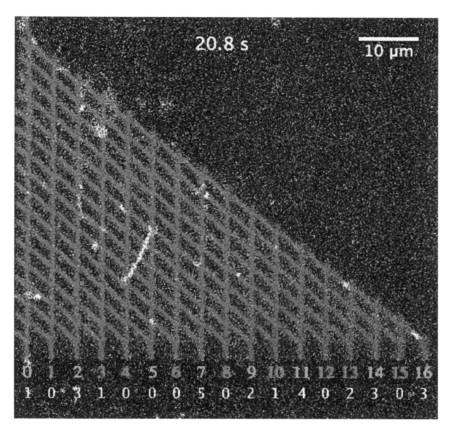

Fig. 2. Fluorescent proteins extracted from rabbit muscle, about a millionth of a millimetre across.

Firstly, the zeal of the quantum computing community for breaking Internet passwords is itself suspect. If a bunch of materials engineers told you about a cutting edge nanotechnology and, on questioning about its potential uses, all they could offer was that it could be used to easily smash every window in the world, most people would raise an eyebrow. Less pejoratively, the use of factorisation for online security is largely a historical accident, since factorisation is not believed to be in the class of 'exponentially hard' problems. We already have myriad security systems based on the purported difficulty of those harder problems, all of which could replace factorisation as the *de rigueur* security technology, rendering the speed advantage of quantum computers essentially insignificant.

Note that none of this has to do with questions of whether quantum computers can scale in practice. There are, to be sure, serious engineering challenges facing their development. These include, *inter alia*, 'decoherence,' increasing the density of signalling and wiring — which is hard to do without degrading the system's stability — and temperature control. There is also the quite real possibility, pointed out by Simon Levin, one of the fathers of computational complexity theory, that we may not understand the laws of quantum physics as well as we think we do, potentially building quantum computers on foundations of theoretical sand.

But that's not the point. If there was a reasonable expectation that quantum computers could, in principle, offer exponential speed-up over regular computers for even a few key computational problems of practical importance, the excitement around the technology would be more than justified and investment in overcoming those engineering problems would be warranted. Unfortunately, based on what we have learned over the past 40 years, that is simply not the case.

On the other hand, there are excellent reasons to continue to study quantum computers. For one thing, they are likely to lead to insights into the laws of quantum physics that we may be able to reach by other experimental means. And quantum computer-like systems could still find an indispensable role in drug discovery, for instance by using quantum computers to simulate quantum molecular processes. Most excitingly, I think, the effort to build and scale quantum computers may teach us about the limits of computing and even, maybe, supply us with a profound new law of physics, which would say that there are some problems for which no computer, of any kind, can find answers in practice, in this world.

So, does the hype around quantum computers fit the medical definition of 'delusion'? Not exactly. For one thing, the *Diagnostic and Statistical Manual of Mental Disorders* tells us that a person cannot be diagnosed as being delusional if the belief in question is one *"ordinarily accepted by other members of the person's culture or subculture."* It's not clear how many believers are needed for a delusional belief at the individual level to escape from the *"folie à..."* diagnostic category, but a cursory Internet search for "quantum computing stock price" makes it clear that this hurdle, wherever it may lie, was passed long ago. When a large number of people come to believe irrational and probably false things based on hearsay, as I suspect is the case of my friend at the Christmas party, that's not considered to be a case of 'clinical' delusion by the psychiatric profession. Instead, we call it something more like 'mass hysteria', which, on my view, is much worse, by dint of lacking the originality and innocence that tend to characterise personal delusions.

[1] Mathematician, physician and engineer, Associate Professor of Computational Mathematics at the Queensland University of Technology and Visiting Professor of Experimental Medicine at the University of Oxford.
[2] Lauren Carter is a London-based painter.

The art of unconventional computing with cellular automata[*]

Genaro J. Martínez,[1] Andrew Adamatzky,[2] Marcin J. Schroeder[3]

The exploration of unconventional computing in its diverse forms is not only, and not primarily a result of the natural human pursuit for innovation but rather a response to challenges faced by the current information technology. Some of these challenges are not new, e.g. the expected end of applicability of Moores Law or the von Neumann bottleneck in the transfer of data between the CPU (central processing unit) and RAM (random-access memory). However, the bottleneck in the past was just a nuisance, but at present the need for massive processing of synaptic weights in the network for machine learning which requires multiple transfer makes this primary tool of AI (artificial intelligence) inefficient and hopeless in the competition with the natural, biological systems of information processing. An example of another challenge of a very different "down to the earth" type is the high energetic cost of machine learning estimated already as a substantial portion of the energetic needs of the industrial societies which in the near future is expected to become the main consumer of energy. Thus, the question about the frugality of nature in the energetic budget for the human or animal brain is worth billions or trillions of the future dollars.

These and other challenges direct the research towards unconventional forms of computing with the special interest in its natural forms identified in living organisms on the one hand, and in the utilization of new, natural, physical phenomena in information processing.

This brings us to a more general and theoretical question overarching the interests in natural forms of information processing about what constitutes the fundamental distinction between the traditional form of computing originating in the theoretical model of a Turing machine, and unconventional, natural computing. One of the possible answers is that the Turing machine model is based on the principle of a one-way, goal-oriented action initiated and controlled by a pre-defined program, while all natural processes are dynamic, *i.e.* they are based on mutual interactions within the processing system and with its environment.[4]

It is possible to consider a modification of the Turing machine model in which instead of the one-way action of the head on the tape the processing is performed by mutual reading and mutual re-writing of the two interacting central components.[5] This model of symmetric inductive machine remains within the Turing limit of computability as soon as the dynamics of interaction is computable, but nothing makes this computability unavoidable.[6]

The shift of the focus on the dynamic, interaction based forms of information processing can be implemented in the most natural way in the information processing in cellular automata where the art of unconventional computing begins. Unconventional and natural computing[7] has the capacity to handle information at an atomic and molecular level, the first stage. A diversity of scientific fields study and research all these ways on continuous and discrete domains. Lines of research can be found in Table 1.

Table 1: Some ways to unconventional computers.

Quantum computers[8]	Reaction-diffusion computers[9]
DNA computers[10]	Hot ice computers[11]
Physarum computers[12]	Collider computers[13]
Optical computers[14]	Thermodynamic computers[15]

In this way, the cellular automata theory conceived by von Neumann in the late 1950s years as a tool of super computation.[16] Von Neumann has been working with primitive and indivisible elements and where this theory offers an inherently and massively computation in parallel. He had discussed that universal Turing machines cannot exploit the process in nature and the universe. This way, the existence of universal constructors becomes essential for the universe.[17] An actual problem is how to control and design reliable components from unreliable organisms.[18] Indeed, this issue is preserved in any unconventional computing architecture. In the literature of cellular automata theory we can see a diversity of designs without any particular architecture. This way, we can think that these machines are adapted for a specific environment. Therefore, we can imagine how these machines

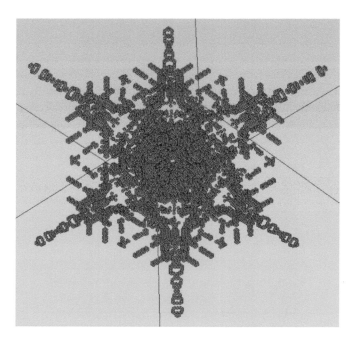

Fig. 1. A three-dimensional projection of cellular automata Life-like rule B4/S9. It is a projection of the two-dimensional Life-like rule *B2/S7*, the *Diffusion Rule*.[20] The rule is a chaotic rule although it supports complex patterns as oscillators, gliders, puffer trains, and an ample diversity of gliders guns. This rule proved logical universal by realisation of computing circuits via collisions between particles. This evolution displays the result of two particles colliding, thus later of 112 steps we can see symmetric complex structures emerging during the evolution, travelling, expanding and interacting with others.

Fig. 2. Three-dimensional projection of the two-dimensional Life-like rule *B2/S7*, the *Diffusion Rule*.[21] The rule is classed as chaotic although it supports complex patterns as oscillators, gliders, puffer trains, and a diversity of gliders guns. The rule is proved logical universal via collisions of particles. This evolution displays the result of two particles in vertical position colliding. The reaction produces a replication of particles periodically in thousands of generations. With time a symmetry is lost and the automaton dynamics becomes chaotic. We call it the cellular automata origin. https://youtu.be/BqTU_uW-zaI

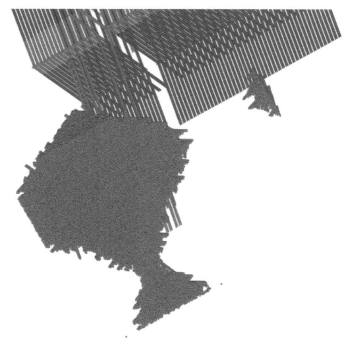

Fig. 3: Three-dimensional projection of a two-dimensional cellular automaton *Life without Dead*, rule *B3/S012345678*. This rule is able to support complex behaviour and logic computability.[22] From random initial conditions you can see the emergence of worms and interesting designs when the worms interact with each other. This evolution start with an initial condition defined by a line of eleven alive cells.

Fig. 4. Metaglider (mesh) designed with the elementary cellular automaton rule 54 synchronising multiple collisions evolving in a ring. It is a three-dimensional projection of a typical two-dimensional evolution. Rule 54 is a logically universal automaton.[23] Logic computation in rule 54 is performed by collisions of particles in its evolution space.

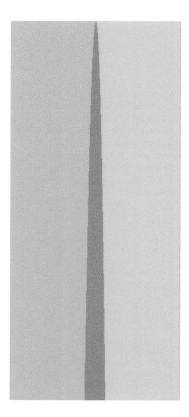

Fig. 5: Two-dimensional representation by colours of a Turing machine that doubles the number of ones as a cellular automaton.[24]

Fig. 6: Two-dimensional representation by colours of a Turing machine that simulates the behaviour of ECA rule 110. The history of the Turing machine is represented as a cellular automaton.[25] The initial condition starts with the string $B*010B*$ showing in two snapshots the evolution to 10,000 steps.

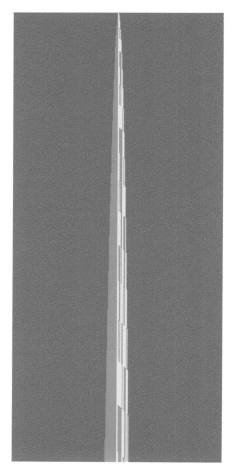

Fig. 7: Two-dimensional representation by colours of a Turing machine that simulates the behaviour of ECA rule 110. The history of the Turing machine is represented as a cellular automaton.[26] The initial condition start with the string $B*010B*$ showing the evolution to 700 steps.

are working simultaneously in nature or the universe, each with its own architecture and environment.[19]

Cellular automata are adequate mathematical machines to represent unicelular computers because of their architectural properties: array of infinite state machines matches arrays of these units. Historically cellular automata theory has been analyzed as supercomputers.[27] On the other hand, cellular automata are explored in an artistic way as was presented in the book *Designing Beauty: the Art of Cellular Automata*.[28]

We can think of *unconventional computers* as the physical devices and *unconventional computing* as the logic medium where these devices work. This way, we can complement the Table 1 with some unconventional computing models listed in the Table 2.

Table 2: Some ways to unconventional computing.

Reversible computing[29]	Conservative computing[30]
Chaotic computing[31]	Crystalline computing[32]
Molecular computing[33]	Tiling computing[34]
Competing patterns computing[35]	Symmetric inductive computing[36]
Soliton computing[37]	Slime mould computing[38]

[1] Escuela Superior de Cómputo, Instituto Politécnico Nacional, México; Unconventional Computing Laboratory, University of the West of England, Bristol, United Kingdom; genaro.martinez@uwe.ac.uk

[2] Unconventional Computing Laboratory, University of the West of England, Bristol, United Kingdom; andrew.adamatzky@uwe.ac.uk

[3] Institute for the Excellence in Higher Education, Tohoku University, Sendai, Japan; schroeder.marcin.e4@tohoku.ac.jp

[4] M. J. SCHROEDER, "From proactive to interactive theory of computation," *The 6th AISB Symposium on Computing and Philosophy: The Scandal of ComputationWhat is Computation?*, 2013, 47-51.

[5] M. J. SCHROEDER, "Towards Autonomous Computation: Geometric Methods of Computing," *APA Newsletter on Philosophy and Computation 15(1)*, 2015, 7-9.

[6] M. BURGIN, "Information Processing by Symmetric Inductive Turing Machines," *Multidisciplinary Digital Publishing Institute Proceedings 47(1)*, 2020, 28.

[7] T. TOFFOLI, "Non-conventional computers," *Encyclopedia of Electrical and Electronics Engineering 14*, 1998 455-471; J. W. MILLS, "The nature of the extended analog computer," *Physica D: Nonlinear Phenomena 237(9)*, 2008, 1235-1256 ; S. B. COOPER, "What Makes A Computation Unconventional?," in G. DODIG-CRNKOVIC & R. GIOVAGNOLI (eds), *Computing Nature: Turing Centenary Perspective*, Berlin/Heidelberg, Springer, 2013, 255-269.

[8] I. L. CHUANG, "IBMs Test-Tube Quantum Computer Makes History," *IBM Research News*, 2001.

[9] A. ADAMATZKY, B. D. L. COSTELLO & T. ASAI, *Reaction-diffusion computers*, Amsterdam, Elsevier, 2005.

[10] G. PAUN, G. ROZENBERG & A. SALOMAA, *DNA computing: new computing paradigms*, Berlin, Springer, 1998.

[11] A. ADAMATZKY, "Hot ice computer," *Physics Letters A 374(2)*, 2009, 264-271.

[12] A. ADAMATZKY, *Physarum machines: computers from slime mould*, London, World Scientific, 2010.

[13] A. ADAMATZKY (ed.), *Advances in Unconventional Computing: Volume 1: Theory*, Cham, Springer, 2016.

[14] T. YATAGAI, "Cellular logic architectures for optical computers," *Applied optics 25(10)*, 1986, 1571-1577.

[15] T. HYLTON, "Thermodynamic Computing: An Intellectual andTechnological Frontier," *Multidisciplinary Digital Publishing Institute Proceedings 47(1)*, 2020, 23.

[16] J. VON NEUMANN, *Theory of Self-reproducing Automata*, ed. A. W. BURKS, Urbana and London, University of Illinois Press, 1966.

[17] J. VON NEUMANN, "Probabilistic logics and the synthesis of reliable organisms from unreliable components," *Automata studies 34*, 1956, 43-98.

[18] *Ibidem*.

[19] A list of computable cellular automata can be found in: *Complex Cellular Automata Repository* https://www.comunidad.escom.ipn.mx/genaro/Complex_CA_repository.html

[20] S. J. MARTÍNEZ, I. M. MENDOZA, G. J. MARTÍNEZ, & S. NINAGAWA, "Universal One-dimensional Cellular Automata Derived from Turing Machines," *International Journal of Unconventional Computing 14(2)*, 2019, 121-138.

[21] *Ibidem*.

[22] D. GRIFFEATH & C. MOORE, "Life without death is P-complete," *Complex Systems 10*, 1996, 437-448.

[23] G. J. MARTÍNEZ, A. ADAMATZKY & H. V. McINTOSH, "Phenomenology of glider collisions in cellular automaton Rule 54 and associated logical gates," *Chaos, Solitons & Fractals 28(1)*, 2006, 100-111.

[24] S. J. MARTÍNEZ, I. M. MENDOZA, G. J. MARTÍNEZ, & S. NINAGAWA, "Universal One-dimensional Cellular Automata Derived from Turing Machines," *op. cit.* ; P. RENDELL,

Turing Machine Universality of the Game of Life, Cham, Springer, 2016.

[25] S. J. Martínez, I. M. Mendoza, G. J. Martínez, & S. Ninagawa, "Universal One-dimensional Cellular Automata Derived from Turing Machines," *op. cit.*

[26] *Ibidem*.

[27] N. Margolus, T. Toffoli & G. Vichniac, "Cellular-automata super- computers for fluid-dynamics modeling," *Physical Review Letters 56(16)*, 1986, 1694; S. Wolfram, "Cellular automaton supercomputing," Center for Complex Systems Research, 1987, online: https://content.wolfram.com/uploads/sites/34/2020/07/cellular-automaton-supercomputing.pdf; A. Adamatzky, *Computing in nonlinear media and automata collectives*, Boca Raton, CRC Press, 2001.

[28] A. Adamatzky & G. J. Martinez (eds), *Designing Beauty: the Art of Cellular Automata*, Cham, Springer, 2016.

[29] C. H. Bennett, "Logical reversibility of computation," *IBM journal of Research and Development 17(6)*, 1973, 525-532; K. Morita, "Reversible computing and cellular automata: A survey," *Theoretical Computer Science 395(1)*, 2008, 101-131.

[30] E. Fredkin & T. Toffoli, "Conservative logic," *International Journal of theoretical physics 21(3-4)*, 1982, 219-253; K. Morita, "A simple universal logic element and cellular automata for reversible computing," in M. Margenstern, Y. Rogozhin (eds), *International Conference on Machines, Computations, and Universality*, Berlin/Heidelberg, Springer, 2001, 102-113.

[31] L. O. Chua, "Chuas circuit: An overview ten years later," *Journal of Circuits, Systems, and Computers 4(02)*, 1994, 117-159.

[32] N. H. Margolus, "Crystalline computation," in A. Hey (ed.), *Feynman and Computation: Exploring the Limits of Computers*, Boca Raton, CRC Press, 1998, 267-305.

[33] T. Sienko, A. Adamatzky & N. Rambidi, *Molecular computing*, Cambridge, MIT Press, 2003.

[34] B. Grünbaum & G. C. Shephard, *Tilings and patterns*, Mineola, Courier Dover Publications, 1987.

[35] G. J. Martínez, A. Adamatzky, K. Morita & M. Margenstern, "Computation with competing patterns in Life-like automaton," in A. Adamatzky (ed.), *Game of Life Cellular Automata*, London, Springer, 2010, 547-572.

[36] M. Burgin, "Information Processing by Symmetric Inductive Turing Machines," *op. cit.*

[37] M. H. Jakubowski, K. Steiglitz & R. Squier, "Computing with solitons: a review and prospectus," in A. Adamatzky (ed.), *Collision-based computing*, London, Springer, 2002, 277-297.

[38] A. Adamatzky, "Slime mould computing," *International Journal of General Systems 44(3)*, 2015, 277-278.

* Free software used to create the simulations in this paper.

- Ready (Tim Hutton, Robert Munafo, Andrew Trevorrow, Tom Rokicki,
https://github.com/gollygang/ready)

- CAviewer (José Antonio Jiménez Amador, Genaro J. Martínez,
https:// www.comunidad.escom.ipn.mx/genaro/Papers/Thesis_files/CAviewer. tar.gz)

- CATM (Sergio Eduardo Juárez Martínez, César Iván Manzano Mendoza, https://www.comunidad.escom.ipn.mx/genaro/Papers/Thesis_files/maquinaTuring.java.tar.gz)

Living wearables from slime mould and fungi

Andrew Adamatzky,[1] Anna Nikolaidou,[2] Antoni Gandia,[3] and Alessandro Chiolerio[4]

Smart wearables, augmented with soft and liquid electronics, can display sensing, responsive and adaptive capabilities, but they cannot self-grow or self-repair. Living organisms colonising a fabric could be a viable alternative. In the present article we briefly review our ideas on implementing living wearables with slime mould and fungi. The living networks of slime mould protoplasmic tubes and fungal mycelium networks can act as distributed sensorial networks, fuse sensorial inputs from wearers and environment, process information in a massive parallel manner and provide responses in benefit of the consortium human-microbe.

Most living creatures have plenty of living wearables: skin, mites, fungal and bacterial colonies colonising the skin, and critters living our hairs. Skin is out living wearable number one. The skin senses, transmit information and, more likely, is capable of distributed decision making. Limitations of the skin are that the skin is not disposable, we cannot change our skin as easy as we can change the pants or socks, sensorial and computational properties of the skins are not easily tunable, attempts to integrate soft and liquid electronics into human skins pose health risks and incompatibility issues. Also it is not acceptable in many cultures to appear in public naked, so a substantial area of our skin should be covered by fabric and thus renders useless for immediate environmental sensing. Traditionally, wearables have acted as covering tools aiming to provide comfort and protection from the elements. They have also constituted semiotic devices, machines for communication[5] and functioned as social mediators and interfaces between our bodies and society.[6] With the emergence of novel and smart materials, the functionality of wearables has been extended, offering new opportunities. Smart materials can be defined as highly engineered materials that respond intelligently to their environment.[7] They are characterized by their ability to detect and respond to stimuli from the environment (such as stress, temperature, moisture, pH, electric or magnetic fields), by a specific change of behaviour, as for instance a colour or shape or form change.[8] Smart materials are often embedded in more conventional materials and applied in a system with microelectronic components and miniaturized technologies.[9]

Smart wearables are devices that are responsive to the wearer, they can sense and process information from the user's body and environment and report results of their analysis as electrical signals.[10] In the last decade, electronics and textiles (e-textiles) have been a fundamental part of smart wearables. Integrating electronics into textile products enables the development of wearable electro-textiles for sensing / monitoring body functions, delivering communication facilities, data transfer, control of the environment, and many other applications.[11] For example, a material surface, such as a common fabric that embeds a nitinol wire (a smart material), can become sensitive and responsive (with visual or kinetic response) according to an external stimulus, like a rise in temperature. This may happen when you wear it, and the increase in body temperature causes the expansion of the fabric.[12] One of the most impacting issues regarding both electron devices and nanocomposite materials is represented by their poor capability to self-repair and grow, to self-organize and adapt to changing environmental conditions. Although smart wearables can display sensing, responsive and adaptive capabilities, they cannot self-grow and self-repair. In addition to

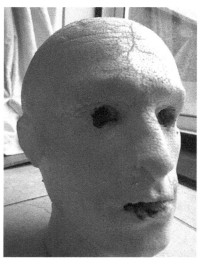

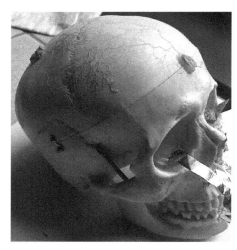

Fig. 1. Live slime mould *Physarum polyceph-alum* growing on a doll. Experiments conducted with A. A.'s daughter, Adriana Adamatzky, in 2010.

Fig. 2. A polyurethane mannequin head colonised by slime mould *Physarum polycephalum.*

Fig. 3. Imitation of scalp innervation with *Physarum polycephalum.*

this, the materials usually used to create the electronic components of the wearables such as metals, plastics and other petroleum-based materials are derived from natural resources, which are limited and non-renewable. Electronic waste or e-waste is one of the emerging problems in developed and developing countries worldwide as it comprises a multitude of components with valuable materials, some containing toxic substances, that can have an adverse impact on human health and the environment.[13] Living organisms could be a viable alternative.

Back in the 2010s we proposed a concept of *extralligence* by growing living slime *Physarum polycephalum* on models of human bodies.[14] We designed, and partly implemented in laboratory conditions with slime mould *Physarum polycephalum*, an intelligent adaptive living network wearable by humans and robots. When grown on 3D bodies (living or inanimate) the living *Physarum* network provides a highly-distributed sensorial structure (light-, electro-magnetic, chemical and tactile sensitivity) with embedded dynamic architecture of massive-parallel computing processors based on geometry of proximity graphs. We have chosen an acellular slime mould *Physarum polycephalum* as amorphous living substrate because Physarum is a living, dynamical reaction

diffusion pattern formation mechanism; Physarum may be considered as equivalent to a membrane bound sub excitable system (excitation stimuli provided by chemo-attractants and chemo-repellents); Physarum may be regarded as a highly efficient and living micro-manipulation and microfluidic transport device; Physarum is sensitive to illumination and AC electric fields and therefore allows for parallel and non-destructive input of information; Physarum represents results of computation by configuration of its body. In experimental laboratory studies, we showed that when inoculated on bare plastic surfaces, Physarum successfully develops an optimal network of protoplasmic tubes spanning sources of attractants while avoiding domains with over threshold concentration of repellents. When exposed to attractants and repellents, Physarum changes patterns of its electrical activity. We experimentally derived a unique one-to-one mapping between a range of selected bioactive chemicals and patterns of oscillations of the slime mould's extracellular electrical potential. This direct and rapid change demonstrates detection of these chemicals in a similar manner to a biological contactless chemical sensor. We believe results could be used in future designs of slime mould based chemical sensors and computers. We also evaluated feasibility of slime-mould based colour sensors by illuminating Physarum with red, green, blue and white colours and analysing patterns of the slime mould's electrical potential oscillations. We defined that the slime mould recognises a colour if it reacts to illumination with the colour by a unique changes in amplitude and periods of oscillatory activity. In laboratory experiments we found that the slime mould recognises red and blue colour. The slime mould does not differentiate between green and white colours. The slime mould also recognises when red colour is switched off. We also mapped colours to diversity of the oscillations: illumination with a white colour increases diversity of amplitudes and periods of oscillations, other colours studied increase diversity either of amplitude or period.

As a proof of concept we designed an experimental laboratory implementation of a slime mould based tactile bristles, where the slime mould responds to repeated deflection of bristle by an immediate high-amplitude spike and a prolonged increase in amplitude and width of its oscillation impulses. We demonstrated that signal strength of the Physarum tactile bristle sensor averages near six for an immediate response and two for a prolonged response.

Despite the sufficient sensorial abilities, the slime mould is rather fragile, highly dependent on environmental conditions and requires particular sources of nutrients. Fungi could, however, make a feasible alternative to the slime mould for the following reasons. Fungal composite materials, normally in form of solid lignocellulosic substrates colonised with the mycelium of filamentous fungi (e.g. *Ganoderma* spp., *Pleurotus* spp., *Trametes* spp.), are an emerging type of biomaterial known by being a robust, reliable and ecologically friendly replacement for conventional building materials and fabrics.[15] Fungi possess almost all the senses used by humans.[16] Fungi sense light, chemicals, gases, gravity and electric fields. Fungi show a pronounced response to changes in a substrate pH,[17] mechanical stimulation,[18] toxic metals,[19] CO_2,[20] and stress hormones.[21] Fungi are known to respond to chemical and physical stimuli by changing patterns of its electrical activity[22] and electrical properties.[23] Thus, wearables made of or incorporating a cellulosic fabric colonised by fungi might act as a large distributed sensorial network.

Fig. 4. Rat whiskers made of living slime mould *Physarum polycephalum.*

To evaluate feasibility of the living fungal wearables, we conducted two sets of laboratory experiments.

In the first set, to assess the sensing potential of fungal wearables, we undertook laboratory experiments on electrical response of a hemp fabric colonised by oyster fungus *Pleurotus ostreatus* to mechanical stretching and stimulation with attractants and repellents.[24] A fabric colonised by the fungus *P. ostreatus* shows distinctive sets of responses to chemical and mechanical stimulation. The response to 50 g load is in the range of 1.5 min which might indicate that rather purely electro-mechanical events take place than reactions involving propagation of calcium waves. The response to stimulation with ethanol is in a range of 7 sec. This would rather indicate physico-chemical damages to hyphae walls and corresponding electrical responses. The increase of frequency of electrical potential oscillation in a response to application of chemo-attractants or nutrients is consistent with previous studies. The increase in amplitude of spiking hours after the application of malt or dextrose might be due to the fungus ingesting the nutrients and transposing them across the wide mycelial network.

In the second set of experiments[25] we experimented with fungal skin. A fungal skin is a thin flexible sheet of a living interwoven, homogeneous, and continuous mycelium made by a filamentous fungus. The skin could be used in future living architectures of adaptive buildings and as a sensing living skin for soft self-growing/adaptive robots. In experimental laboratory studies, we demonstrated that the fungal skin is capable of recognising mechanical and optical stimulation. The skin reacts differently to loading of a weight, removal of the weight,

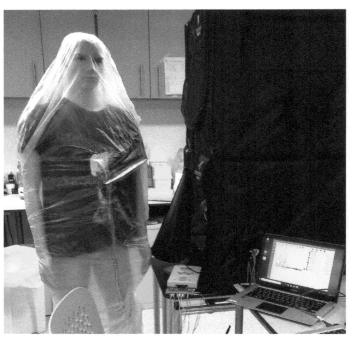

Fig. 5. A photo of experimental setup showing a hemp pad colonised with fungi, attached to a T-shirt with electrodes and recording equipment.

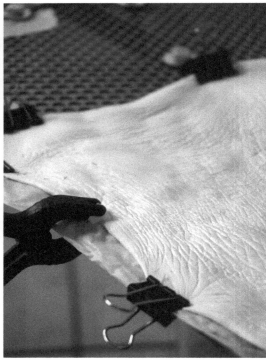

Fig. 6. The fungal skin shows animal type wrinkles.

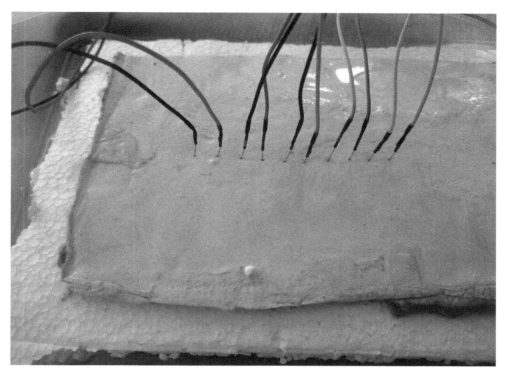

Fig. 7. Pairs of differential electrodes inserted in the fungal skin to record electrical response of the fungal skin to mechanical and optical stimulation.

and switching illumination on and off. These are the first experimental evidences that fungal materials can be used not only as mechanical skeletons in architecture and robotics but also as intelligent skins capable of recognition of external stimuli and sensorial fusion.

Living wearables offer a new spectrum of performance possibilities such as reactiveness, adaptiveness, and sensing capabilities. They are harmless to the environment, biodegradable and they can even nurture the cultivation of new materials in their end of life. The living material provides a unique opportunity for the wearables to be programmable by guiding the growth, controlling the nutrients and setting up the conditions in which the wearable can be created. Their ability to self-repair and self-grow makes them one of the most promising. Future studies can be focused on better understanding of electrical communication and stimulation in fungi and other microbes (advancements in biocomputation), development of biological sensors able to report slight changes in physico-environmental conditions and biochemical traces, biological sentient

clothing that responds to the environment, self-sustaining and self-healing clothing and parchments grown *in situ*, exoskins and exoskeletons that symbiotically interact with the user, cross-over synergistic interactions between biological entities and electronic circuits or machines (advancements in biorobotics and biomechanoids).

[1] Professor in Unconventional Computing, UWE, Bristol, UK.

[2] Senior Lecturer in Architecture, UWE, Bristol, UK.

[3] Leading Researcher at MOGU, Italy.

[4] Leading Researcher at IIT, Torino, Italy.

[5] U. Eco, *Travels in Hyperreality*, New York, Mariner Books, 1986.

[6] M. Barnard, *Fashion Theory: An Introduction*, London, Routledge, 2014.

[7] M. Addington, D. Schodek, *Smart Materials and New Technologies. For Architecture and Design Professions*, Oxford, Architectural Press-Elsevier, 2005.

[8] M. Ferrara, M. Bengisu, *Materials that Change Color. Smart Materials, Intelligent Design*, Cham, Springer, 2013.

[9] M. FERRARA, "Smart Experience in Fashion Design: A speculative analysis of smart material systems applications," *Arts Basel 8*, 2019, 1-11.

[10] A. ADAMATZKY, A. NIKOLAIDOU, A. GANDIA, A. CHIOLERIO, and M. M. DEHSHIBI," Reactive fungal wearable," arXiv preprint arXiv:2009.05670 (2020).

[11] X. T TAO, *Wearable Electronics and Photonics*, Cambridge, Woodhead Publishing Limited and Textile Institute Abington, 2005.

[12] M. FERRARA, M. BENGISU, *Materials that Change Color*, op. cit.

[13] S. NEEDHIDASAN, M. SAMUEL, R. CHIDAMBARAM, "Electronic waste – an emerging threat to the environment of urban India," *Journal of Environmental Health Science and Engineering 12(1)*, 2014, 36.

[14] A. ADAMATZKY & T. SCHUBERT, "Slime Extralligence: Developing a Wearable Sensorial and Computing Network with Physarum polycephalum," UWE Research Repository 927012, 2013.

[15] F. V. APPELS, S. CAMERE, M. MONTALTI, E. KARANA, K. M. JANSEN, J. DIJKSTERHUIS, P. KRIJGSHELD, H. A. WOSTEN, "Fabrication factors influencing mechanical, moisture-and water-related properties of mycelium-based composites," *Materials & Design 161*, 2019, 64-71; M. JONES, A. GANDIA, S. JOHN, A. BISMARCK, "Leather-like material biofabrication using fungi," *Nature Sustainability*, 2020. https://doi.org/10.1038/s41893-020-00606-1

[16] Y.-S. BAHN, C. XUE, A. IDNURM, J. C. RUTHERFORD, J. HEITMAN, M. E. CARDENAS, "Sensing the environment: lessons from fungi," *Nature Reviews Microbiology 5*, 2007, 57.

[17] I. M. VAN AARLE, P. A. OLSSON, B. SODERSTROM, "Arbuscular mycorrhizal fungi respond to the substrate ph of their extraradical mycelium by altered growth and root colonization," *New Phytologist 155*, 2002, 173-182.

[18] C. KUNG, "A possible unifying principle for mechanosensation," *Nature 436(7051)*, 2005, 647.

[19] M. FOMINA, K. RITZ, G. M. GADD, "Negative fungal chemotropism to toxic metals," *FEMS Microbiology Letters 193*, 2000, 207-211.

[20] Y.-S. BAHN, F. A. MUHLSCHLEGEL, "Co2 sensing in fungi and beyond," *Current opinion in microbiology 9*, 2006, 572-578.

[21] K. T. HOWITZ, D. A. SINCLAIR, "Xenohormesis: sensing the chemical cues of other species," *Cell 133*, 2008, 387-391.

[22] S. OLSSON, B. HANSSON, "Action potential-like activity found in fungal mycelia is sensitive to stimulation," *Naturwissenschaften 82*, 1995, 30-31; A. ADAMATZKY, "On spiking behaviour of oyster fungi pleurotus djamor," *Scientific reports 8*, 2018, 1-7; A. ADAMATZKY, A. GANDIA, A. CHIOLERIO, "Fungal sensing skin," arXiv preprint arXiv:2008.09814 (2020).

[23] A. E. BEASLEY, A. L. POWELL, A. ADAMATZKY, "Fungal photosensors," arXiv preprint arXiv:2003.07825 (2020).

[24] A. ADAMATZKY, A. NIKOLAIDOU, A. GANDIA, A. CHIOLERIO, and M. M. DEHSHIBI, "Reactive fungal wearable," op. cit.

[25] *Ibidem.*

Brain Lego
Toy Computing with Lego Bricks

Stefan Höltgen[1]

"HIRNLEGOHIRNLEGOHIRNLEGOLEGOLEGO
HIRNLEGOLEGOLEHIRNLEGOLEGOLEGO
HIRNLEGOLEGOLEGOHIRNLEGOLEGOLEGO"

(*Einstürzende Neubauten*, Hirnlego, 1989)

"I have always had a predominantly visual approach to my environment. This is also probably why I never pursued music. This perhaps one-sided talent was also evident in the construction of my computer models; here, too, I preferred mechanical and electromechanical constructions and left the electronics to others who were better qualified."[2]
In this quote, computer pioneer Konrad Zuse describes his tinkering with construction kits he played with as a boy and a teenager from his viewpoint as an engineer. He used those kits in the 1920s to build all sorts of things with them: (award winning) models of cranes and excavators, spare parts for his bike, and mechanical household aids. Later on, when his computers were already working electronically, he used the thought pattern for a new system of self-reproducing machines.[3]

This mechanical thinking of computer functions has a long tradition reaching back into the Middle Ages: from Ramon Llullu's book *Ars Magna* published in 1305 where a theological 'converter' for Muslims to become Christians is drafted, to Leibniz' *Machina arithmeticae dyadicae* from 1679 (a mechanism to calculate with binary numbers) — both remained "paper machines" — through to the mechanical and electromechanical logical machines of the 19th and 20th centuries,[4] culminating in Claude Shannon's switching algebra from 1937. All of these drafts were based on the idea to make calculation and computation not only logically but also mechanically constructible.

From our present-day perspective, some of these drafts appear more like toys than serious calculators; toys that merely show the principles of computation but are not very suitable for actual usage. This view also has to do with the fact that those prototypes show their material and epistemological toy characteristics:

they are often built from construction kits (for children and youth) or from everyday objects — according to the "Baukastenprinzip" ("kit principle"),[5] using heuristic design procedures, trial and error, and learning by doing.

The invitation to *think while tinkering* ("thinkering")[6] seems to be a basic principle of both logic and kit toying because both make it possible to comprehend/handle complex phenomena. This logic (the two-valued sentential logic, inaugurated in the 3rd century B.C. from Aristotle) is the timeless and non-spatial basis of all our thinking. It provides the transcendental basic structure of truth-apt propositions which are the foundation of our everyday thinking, actions, science, playing, ... This reality is formalized in logics: propositions become tokens that can hold a truth value (true/false — no third option) and can be combined with junctors (and, or, if-then, not, ...) to complex sentences.

A sentence like *"Tonight I'll go to the movies or I will read a book"* can be formalized as *p v q* where *p* means *"I'll go to the cinema"*, *q* means *"I'll read a book"*, and the *v* stands for the logical OR (not *either-or* since I can read my book in the cinema as well). Since each of these sentences can be true (t) or false (f), their or-combination can also be true or false. Ludwig Wittgenstein, following the system of Chrysippos of Soloi (279-206 B.C.), inaugurated a notation table to show the possible iterations:[7]

p	v	q
t	t	t
t	t	f
f	t	t
f	f	f

The fact that topics of thoughts and deeds can be formalized and written down in this manner fueled the speculation that logic does not always have to be transcendental but can be transferred from the realm of the symbols into the real. The mention of the logical machines in the beginning proves this to be true: propositions can become variables and variables can be transformed into versatile rods within a logical-mechanical design.

With the help of these machines logic, and only logic, can be automatized. To transform logical machines into computers that can calculate anything calculable, a third transformation must happen: propositions must become variables again and truth values must become numbers. This transformation was accomplished by George Boole in the late 19th century when he invented an algebra on the basis of Leibniz' system of binary numbers. Here, the truth values of t became 1, f became 0, and the logical junctors became arithmetic operators: and as *, or as + and not as -. Only three operators were sufficient to build all of the 16 possible junctors as the logician Charles Sanders Peirce proved in 1880.

To implement those logical functions into machines, merely a process of mental reinterpretation had to happen where a real state is read as a mathematical cipher. The real basis could be different electrical currents, pressure

differences of air or liquid, the presence or absence of a sound (or two different frequencies) — or the locomotion of mechanical parts. To say *"computers do understand only ones and zeros"* means: all of their computation is based on binary switching logic on whatever substrate. This primitive foundation is capable of an enormous complexity which can be determined in modern computers. They are only using more, faster, and smaller logical gates but work on the same regime.

The incrementation of complexity that leads to all the emergent effects of modern computing is nearly incomprehensible let alone can

Lectron

Fig. 1. Braun Lectron (top center), Dr. NIM (bottom left), 'Denken mit Lego' (bottom right).

be reenacted with macroscopic materials. To get an understanding of the logic behind those computing machines, it would have to be made visible again — by magnification, spatialization, and deceleration. This is where a fundamental review of computer history starts that can be considered as didactics: the handiness of toys that led to the construction of the first computers nearly one century ago can be used to get an understanding of today's ancestor. That is mainly because their fundamental principles are the same. Even the didactic is not new.

As early as the 1950s, toys[8] were built that made logical computer functions comprehensible/tangible (Fig. 1). The advent of digital computers in children's rooms transformed the didactics into a hands-on comprehension. This was realized by the use of kit systems that allowed implementing logical values and junctors in many different ways: electronic kits[9] (with newly designed "digital expansions", fig. 1, middle) and building bricks that facilitate the construction of mechanism — like Fischertechnik[10] or Lego.

"Denken mit Lego" (Thinking with Lego) paved the way for these 'brick didactics': a lego kit with a book companion where two mathematicians suggested *"funny games with logics and set theory"*[11] to *"provide experiences of the cohesion between propositional logics and set theory to children."*[12] Lego bricks were particularly suitable for this and could also be used to explain *"different bases of number systems"*[13] — especially of the binary system. By playing so-called "goal games" (91) logical junctors should be 'passed through' mentally: *"Any passway walked through provides a meaningful experience to the pupils"*[14] — the authors note before they show a diagram of the paths for *p v q* resp. *p ^ q*.

Using the lego brick to actually convert such 'thinking paths' into operational mechanisms only came to the minds of Lego players in the course of the last decade. Initially, they had to try the 'misuse of toy devices' and convert all sorts of things[15] into computers — just to see if it was possible. Computers themselves had provoked such hacking — unfinished gadgets that were just waiting to be transformed into usable tools by *programming* them. The hackers had approached them down to their hardware substrates. So, why not shift away this last symbolic historic and spatial border and expose their basic functions to the hacker creativity? Just to explore what computers are made of …

This is why so many Lego projects can be found today that introduce computers as calculating machines,[16] as theoretical constructions (Turing Machines),[17] and as logical networks — for replication with bricks. Logical AND, OR, and NOT gates can be easily assembled

with only a few Lego bricks. (Only adding some rubber bands to help the gates return to their default state.) Instructions for "Lego Lever Logic"[18] gates can be recommended because they are easy to combine with each other to larger structures.

The gate's switching states can be recognized by the length of their levers: a long lever at the input stands for 0, a short lever stands for 1 — vice versa at the gate's output. Connecting the levers of a gate's output to another gate's input enables it to transmit a signal from the first to the second gate. Using some crafting skills, a stable construction of Lego gates that is anything but *"crude and [...] unworkable"*[19] can be built that provides complex working 'digital-mechanic' arithmetic circuits — like an adder that only utilizes AND, OR, and NOT gates. Such constructions are mostly build with the trial-and-error method: re-thinking and re-plugging bricks again and again — which can be seen as an re-enactment of Konrad Zuse's mechanical working Z1 computer architecture.[20]

Such projects can show how the abstract ideas of digital switching circuits become comprehensible hands-on. There are no boundaries for the creator's creativity and the circuit's complexity. The mechanical and material point of view of the formal principles of computing can help to not only comprehend the fundamentals of actual computer technology but also offers new ways of building computer technology by understanding the metaphor of "modular systems"[21] literally: *"Logic gates can be built in many ways. In mechanical computers they can be constructed by gear systems. In molecular computers they can be represented chemically."*[22] These and even more 'alien' concepts are discussed within the realm of unconventional computing. Toy computing with Lego and other construction kits lines up into this experimental computer science — and enables an epistemological view on its historical and material sources.[23]

Fig. 2: Lego Lever Logic: AND, OR, NOT Gates (left), NAND gate (combined from AND and NOT) (right).

[1] Humboldt-Universität zu Berlin, Institut für Musikwissenschaft und Medienwissenschaft, Bereich Medienwissenschaft, Georgenstraße 47, D-10117 Berlin.

[2] K. ZUSE, *The Computer – My Life*, Berlin/Heidelberg, Springer, 1993, 9.

[3] N. EIBISCH, *Selbstreproduzierende Maschinen. Konrad Zuses Montagestraße SRS 72 und ihr Kontext*, Wiesbaden, Springer/Vieweg, 2016, 21.

[4] Cf. M. GARDNER, *Logic machines and diagrams*, New York/Toronto/London, McGraw-Hill, 1958.

[5] N. EIBISCH, *Selbstreproduzierende Maschinen, op. cit.*

[6] E. HUHTAMO, "Thinkering with Media. On the Art of Paul deMarinis," in I. BEIRER, S. HIMMELSBACH, C. SEIFFARTH (eds), *Paul DeMarinis: Buried in Noise*, Heidelberg, Kehrer, 2010, 33-46.

[7] L. WITTGENSTEIN, *Tractatus logico-philosophicus*, trans. D. F. PEARS & B. F. McGUINNESS, London/New York, Routledge, 2002, 38.

[8] http://txt3.de/brainlego1

[9] http://txt3.de/brainlego2

[10] http://txt3.de/brainlego3

[11] H. FREUND, P. SORGER, *Denken mit LEGO. Vergnügliche Denkspiele für Logik und Mengenlehre*, Freiburg/Basel/Wien, Herder. (Quotes translation by S. Höltgen.)

[12] *Ibidem*.

[13] *Ibid*.

[14] *Ibid*.

[15] "Dominoes even make for a fun gate implementation (albeit one that can only be run once)." J. SEIFFERTT, *Digital Logic for Computing*, Cham, Springer, 2017, 76.

[16] http://txt3.de/brainlego4

[17] http://txt3.de/brainlego5

[18] http://txt3.de/brainlego6

[19] J. SEIFFERTT, *Digital Logic for Computing, op. cit.*

[20] Cf. K. ZUSE, *The Computer – My Life*, Berlin/Heidelberg, Springer, 2007, 35.

[21] H. G. FRANK, B. S. MEDER, *Einführung in die kybernetische Pädagogik*, München, dtv, 1971, 102-107; N. EIBISCH, *Selbstreproduzierende Maschinen, op. cit.*, 36-45.

[22] J. SEIFFERTT, *Digital Logic for Computing, op. cit.*

[23] http://txt3.de/brainlego7

Intelligent technological tattoos.
Science, Art and Technology on and under the skin

Catarina Pombo Nabais[1]

"The most profound in man is the skin."
Paul Valéry

This article explores the most recent kind of tattoos: the intelligent technological tattoos. These tech-tattoos have the capacity of sensing, measuring, analysing and emitting data about the body's biochemistry through signs and colours inscribed in and on the skin, depending if they are done in the body with conductive ink or if they are worn on the skin. Even if still temporary — because conductivity is lost through skin's natural resistance —, tech-tattoo aims at becoming a daily device.

What if we could transform our skin into the most intelligent, smart, interactive technological device? What if our skin would be able to exhibit all kinds of internal data about our body's biochemistry and nervous system? What if our skin, our thin and fragile surface, was the most profound and powerful part of our body?

The skin is the biggest organ of the body. It is the body's frontier, its physical limit and delimitation, its surface, its border. The skin functions as a membrane-wall of protection as well as an opaque boundary concealing the body from the outside. But the skin is also what exposes the body to the exterior world, what opens up the body, connecting it with the outside. Thus, paradoxically, the skin is at the same time what encloses and what opens up the body. For centuries, the only way to see the interior of the body, underneath the skin, was by anatomical interventions done to dead corpses. Only recently, medicine was able to overcome the opacity of the skin by using technologies such as X-ray, Ultra-sound, Computed tomography (CT) or magnetic resonance imaging (MRI), among many others. Nowadays, another big step is being done. What was available only through medical exams may now be easily shared by technological tattoo which emits data through signs and colours inscribed in and on the skin. Through tech-tattoo, skin becomes the body's biggest exposure. The enclosed mysterious body is now transformed in pure transparency as if body becomes naked.

To be or not to be human. That is the question.

Nowadays, it is interesting to realize that one of the most ancient practices of body inscription such as tattooing[2] becomes a recent area of research in science and technology. Many laboratories have taken tattooing into the world of artificial intelligence. Close to a science-fiction scenario, tech-tattoo is now on the way of becoming the most intelligent body device, transforming humans into cyborgs. Made of nanotech electronic components such as electro-conducive ink or fabric tape, bio-sensors, curvy wires, thermo-chromic ink, and sometimes also imitation gold leaf metal inscribed over the skin, technological tattoo is exponentially expanding. Even if still temporary because conductivity is lost through skin's natural resistance, tech-tattoo aims at becoming a permanent bio-smart device.

There are two kinds of tech-tattoos nowadays. One is inscribed in the skin, as a traditional tattoo but with a special ink that is linked to Wi-Fi devices. A recent yet already famous example is a tattoo which can reproduce a sound that is previously memorized in the drawing.

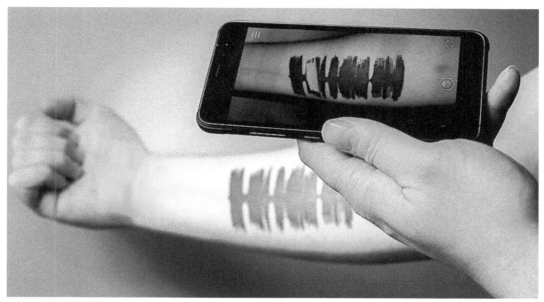

Fig. 1. In the *Skin Motion* website, there are some recommendations about the *Soundwave tattoo*: it should be no larger than 6 inches or 150 mm to be fully captured by the camera on the phone, it should be done in a flat surface such as the inner-forearm and it should be placed where one can easily hold the phone to play the tattoo back with the *Skin Motion* app. Image credit: Sarah Tew/CNET.[3]

First, an audio clip is uploaded in the website of *Skin Motion* company and then a certified artist will grave it in the skin as a traditional tattoo but with a conductive ink which is connected to the *Skin Motion* app. The way this app scans the tattoo is similar to some apps that scan QR codes. It is called the *Soundwave Tattoo*™ and it was invented in April 2017, by the tattoo artist Nate Siggard, who shared his invention in a video on Facebook that immediately went viral (over 150 million views during the first month). He then created the *Skin Motion* company, specialized in what he expresses as "personalized Augmented Reality Tattoos."[4] (Fig. 1.) The other kind is a tattoo that is glued over the skin and disappears by washing like the fake tattoos that some kids use. Titled *Duo skin*, *Double Skin* or *Tech Tat*,[5] this temporary tech-tattoo belongs to a new generation of flexible nano materials. The future perspective is that they will become a daily life's device (Fig. 2).

Due to the fast-technological evolution and to their cheap and easy process of fabrication, tech-tattoos are being appropriate for an enormous range of concrete purposes having direct impact in daily life. They may have utilitarian purposes such as providing a payment system, tracking individuals in space, or giving instructions to the Wi-Fi devices to which the tattooed subject may be connected. Or they may have a deeper bio-medical-political dimension when, e.g. they make possible measuring the body's temperature, the heart beats, the level of alcohol or the blood pressure, supervising fitness, computing sleep patterns, in a word, monitoring vital, bio-metric data.

There are at least two main methodologies for producing smart tattoos: synthetic biology and nanotechnology. Synthetic biology operates skin genetic manipulation. It may produce a cell that gets coloured when it detects bio-chemistry changes in the body, thus rendering the tattoo visible and coloured. Nanotechnology manipulates matter on the nano scale (1-100 nano meters). Instead of using solid pigment particles like in standard tattoos, nanotechnology uses hollow microcapsules which can be filled with diverse materials, depending on the tattoo function.

All these technological advances on smart tattoos, are used for military purposes by detecting poisons in the air, by discovering pathogens in soldiers or by recognizing when soldiers are stressed or hurt. Tech-tattoo has already and will have further in the future a great value in medical uses. One example: Harvard Medical School and MIT have been developing a project called "Dermal Abyss." This project aims at identifying the levels of glucose and sodium in the blood to help in diabetes medical care. In this case, tattoo is made with a smart ink that contains colorimetric and fluorescent biosensors which transforms the skin into a colour sign emitter of biochemical changes in the body. Depending on blood glucose, sodium or pH levels, the skin emits various shades of colours. It can become pink or purple depending on the pH level, it can go from blue to brown depending on blood glucose, or even fluorescent under ultraviolet light depending on sodium level (Fig. 3).

Another example: Carson Burns, a researcher in molecular nanotechnology at the University of Colorado, is developing a tattoo that goes from invisible to coloured spots when the skin is overexposed to sun light and to UV rays. Powered by solar energy, this tech-tattoo has in its micro particles an UV sensitive colour changing dye. Working as an alert, appearing only when the skin is overexposed to UV radiation, this tattoo may help in the sunburn or cancer prevention (Fig. 4).

To be or not to be surveilled. That is the other question.

Technological tattoo is incredibly expanding. However, it is important to notice that the investment being done in this kind of technology

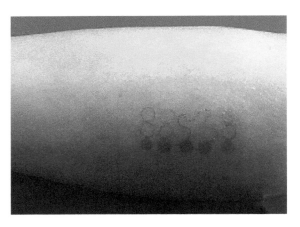

Fig. 2. Tech-tattoo made with one-atom size, two-dimensional single layer of graphene. Contrary to regular temporary tattoos, graphene tattoo is almost transparent. Image credit: **Shideh Kabiri Ameri, Deji Akinwande, et al.**

from international companies allied with research centres and science laboratories makes the biopolitical power of tech-tattoo very clear. In a control society as we already live in, tech-tattoo is a big step into the reinforcement of individual's control. With tech-tattos, data emission on individuals' lives is done, not just from the cell phone but from bio-nano-sensors of a body artificial device. The cell phone — which is already a smart tool — is able to spread lots of information about our movements, GPS location, tastes, social milieus, number of daily steps, etc. But the tech-tattoo with its bio-nano-sensors goes deeply by informing about the diseases, the genetics, the very chemistry of each individual. And in

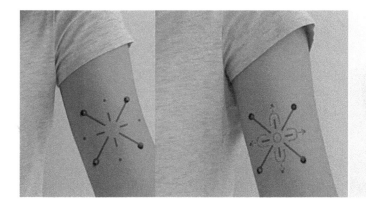 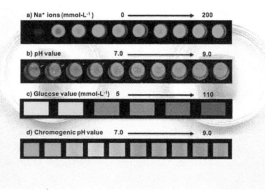

Fig 3. On the left, *Dermal Abyss* tattoo. On the right, *Dermal Abyss* colour palette. Both photos are from Nan Jiang, postdoctoral fellow at the School of Engineering and Applied Sciences at Harvard University, who has been working at Harvard Medical School undertaking research on nano biotechnology and biosensors for the *Dermal Abyss* project.

Fig. 4. When UV ray light illuminates the skin (on the right), two blue spots appear on the skin (on the left). Both images are taken from TED talk by Carlson Burns.[6]

providing all this multitude of inner, intimate data, tech-tattoo is in total, instantaneous, and permanent connection with the control technologies around us. Besides emitting data, tech-tattoo is also capable of sensing, measuring, and analysing data. Therefore, we may say that "bio-wearable" tech-tattoo turns the body into a digital cyborg exempted from privacy and, moreover, it transforms the body into a bio-tech surface, a smart and quantifiable canvas. Tech-tattoo is thus a truly control device, which can be easily used by power structures.

In "Post-Scriptum on Control Societies" (1990), Gilles Deleuze analyses the shift from the disciplinary society, which extends from the 18th century to the last decades of the 20th century,

to the control society. This shift happens with the emergence of a diffuse world-capitalism aligned with digital devices able to control individuals in their personal activities and consumption habits. In disciplinary societies described by Michel Foucault,[8] all activities were framed in specific architectonic buildings (schools, hospitals, fabrics, etc.) where individuals were fixed in space and time and could be controlled by central structures. Time and space dictated life, in a transcendent mode. Now, in control societies, individuals become digital nomads. No matter where and when, they are flowing in a global web, subjected to an immanent control.

Deleuze seems to be terribly prescient. In the early 90s, two years before Tom Barnes Lee's

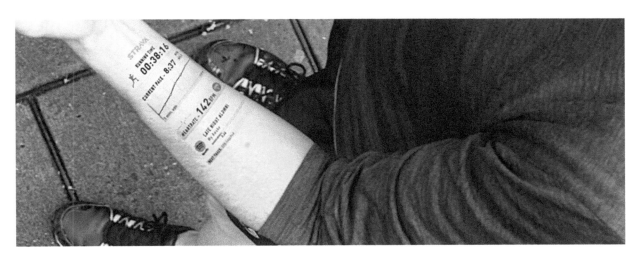

Fig. 5. Software company *Chaotic Moon* has developed a tech-tattoo that is implanted into a person's arm, capable of registering the financial and medical information of the tattooed individual. According to *Chaotic Moon*'s hardware creative technologist, Eric Schneider, "*with the tech tattoo you can carry all your information on your skin and when you want your credit card information or your ID, you can pull that up automatically through the system.*"[7] Image credit: www.emergeinteractive.com.

creation of the World Wide Web, Deleuze stresses that the subject produced by a control society is a navigator (a surfer) in a global floating world: *"The disciplinary man was a discontinuous producer of energy, but the subject of control is undulating, in orbit, in a continuous network. Everywhere surfing has already replaced the old sports."*[9]

Now, the body is no longer an independent and autonomous entity, living almost anonymously, as it used to be in disciplinary societies. In control societies, the body becomes an entity within the global digital world. It is part of an infinite database of power structures which, through digital devices, have a perfect and total command of the individual's life, even if only while taking a walk in the street. Modern body has become the locus of constant social management, a satellite unit or — precisely by means of tech-tattoo — even a control device in itself.

Unlike Jeremy Bentham's Panopticon, with a centralized focal point from which the disciplined activity of individuals is monitored, in control society, a diffuse, widespread, and decoded matrix of information controls the individuals' body and behaviour all the time and everywhere. The "Panopticon" becomes a "Superpanopticon": more subtle, invisible, close and so intimate that it turns to be almost indifferent. We know that we are being watched, but we are not forced to be in a specific place. On the contrary, we are encouraged to move and not to worry about being watched. This normalization of surveillance has become immanent to the modern body and will become even more internalized with the spread of tech-tattoo.

[1] PhD in Philosophy from the University of Paris 8 (2007), researcher at the Faculdade de Ciências da

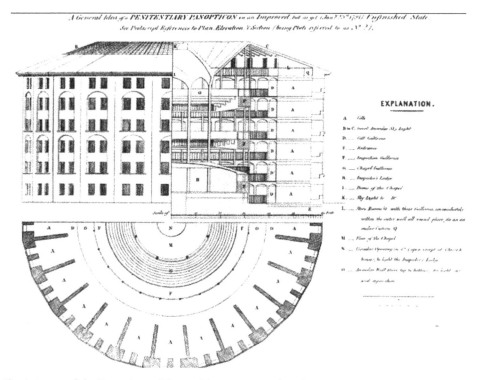

Fig. 6. Image of the Panopticon elaborated by Jeremy Bentham in 1791 in his work *Panopticon; Or, The Inspection-House*.[10]

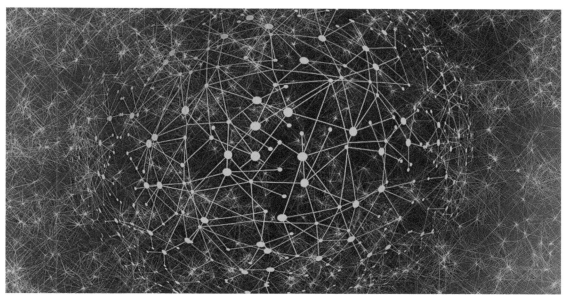

Fig. 7. Iconic representation of the web. Image credit: https://pixabay.com/

Universidade de Lisboa, Departamento de História e Filosofia das Ciências. Integrated member of the Centro de Filosofia das Ciências, Universidade de Lisboa, Campo Grande 1749-016 Lisboa, Portugal. Email: ccnabais@fc.ul.pt.

This work is financed by national funds through FCT – Fundação para a Ciência e a Tecnologia, I.P., within the scope of the Norma Transitória – DL57/2016/CP1479/CT0067 and the Norma Transitória – DL57/2016/CP1479/CT0065.

[2] The most ancient tattooed body dates from 5000 years ago, but tattoos are known to be practiced since the Upper Paleolithic period (10-30 000 years ago). Cf. C. TALIAFERRO & M. ODDEN, "Tattoos and the tattooing arts in perspective: an overview and some preliminary observations," in R. ARP (ed.), *Tattoos: philosophy for everyone: I Ink, Therefore I Am*, Oxford, John Wiley & Sons, 2012, 4. For a more detailed analysis of tattoo throughout history and its meanings, see my article "The most profound is the skin – the power of tattoos," in D. HONORATO, A. GIANNAKOULOPOULOS (eds), *Taboo-Transgression-Transcendence in Art & Science, Proceedings of the 10th Interdisciplinary Conference and Audiovisual Arts Festival, Department of Audio & Visual Arts – Ionian University of Corfu, Greece*, Corfu, Ionian University Press, 2017, 128-148.

[3] In B. VANGELDER, A. NUNES, "Skin Motion app turns my tattoo into sound waves," https://www.cnet.com/news/skin-motion-app-soundwave-tattoo-i-tried-it/

[4] In *Skin Motion. Tattoos brought to life*, https://skinmotion.com/soundwave-tattoos/.

[5] In *Chaotic Moon*, https://www.youtube.com/watch?v=9i-FuTaqD4fM&t=29s.

[6] See TED talk by Carlson Burns:

https://www.ted.com/talks/carson_bruns_could_a_tattoo_help_you_stay_healthy/transcript#t-403948. For further information, see J. L. BUTTERFIELD, S. P. KEYSER, K. V. DIKSHIT, H. KWON, M. I. KOSTER, and C. J. BRUNS, "Solar Freckles: Long-Term Photochromic Tattoos for Intradermal Ultraviolet Radiometry," in *ACS Nano* 14(10), 2020, 13619–13628, https://pubs.acs.org/doi/10.1021/acsnano.0c05723.

[7] In https://newyork.cbslocal.com/2016/01/29/tech-tattoos-chaotic-moon/.

[8] See M. FOUCAULT, *Discipline and Punish. The Birth of Prison*, trans. A. SHERIDAN, New York, Vintage Books, 1995.

[9] G. DELEUZE, "Post-scriptum sur les sociétés de contrôle," in *Pourparlers*, Paris, Minuit, 1990, 244.

[10] In J. BOWRING (ed.), *The Works of Jeremy Bentham*, Edinburgh, William Tait, 1838-1843, vol. 4, 172.

About the authors

ANDREW ADAMATZKY. Professor, Unconventional Computing Laboratory, University of the West of England, Bristol, United Kingdom; andrew.adamatzky@uwe.ac.uk.

SELIM G. AKL. School of Computing, Queen's University, Kingston, Ontario K7L 3N6, Canada, akl@cs.queensu.ca.

MARK BURGIN. UCLA, Los Angeles, CA 90095, USA.

ALESSANDRO CHIOLERIO. Leading Researcher at Istituto Italiano di Tecnologia, Center for Sustainable Future Technologies, Torino, Italy; University of West of England, Unconventional Computing Lab, Bristol, UK.

ANTONI GANDIA. Leading Researcher at MOGU, Italy.

PIER LUIGI GENTILI. Physical Chemistry Professor focused on Complex Systems, Department of Chemistry, Biology, and Biotechnology, Università degli Studi di Perugia, Italy.

STEFAN HÖLTGEN. Humboldt-Universität zu Berlin, Institut für Musikwissenschaft und Medienwissenschaft, Bereich Medienwissenschaft, Georgenstraße 47, D-10117 Berlin. stefan@hoeltgen.org

ZORAN KONKOLI. Professor at Chalmers University of Technology, Goteborg, Sweden.

OLGA KOSHELEVA. University of Texas at El Paso, El Paso, TX 79968, USA, olgak@utep.edu.

VLADIK KREINOVICH. University of Texas at El Paso, El Paso, TX 79968, USA, vladik@utep.edu.

BRUCE MACLENNAN. Associate Professor Emeritus, Department of Electrical Engineering & Computer Science, University of Tennessee.

GENARO J. MARTÍNEZ. Escuela Superior de Cómputo, Instituto Politécnico Nacional, México; Unconventional Computing Laboratory, University of the West of England, Bristol, United Kingdom; genaro.martinez@uwe.ac.uk.

RICHARD MAYNE. Unconventional Computing Laboratory, University of the West of England, Bristol BS16 1QY, United Kingdom. Richard.Mayne@uwe.ac.uk.

KENICHI MORITA. Professor Emeritus, Hiroshima University, Higashi-Hiroshima, Japan.

DAN V. NICOLAU, JR. Mathematician, physician and engineer, Associate Professor of Computational Mathematics at the Queensland University of Technology and Visiting Professor of Experimental Medicine at the University of Oxford.

ANNA NIKOLAIDOU. Senior Lecturer in Architecture, UWE, Bristol, UK.

IRINA PETROVA. Affiliated artist in the Unconventional Computing, Lab, UWE, Bristol, UK.

CATARINA POMBO NABAIS. Department of History and Philosophy of Sciences, Faculty of Sciences, University of Lisbon, Portugal and Integrated member of the Centre of Philosophy of Sciences of the University of Lisbon, ccnabais@fc.ul.pt.

DAWID PRZYCZYNA. PhD student (physics), guitarist, darbuka player, AGH University of Science and Technology, Kraków, Poland.

NANCY SALAY. Associate Professor at the Department of Philosophy, Queen's University, Canada.

MARCIN J. SCHROEDER. Institute for the Excellence in Higher Education, Tohoku University, Sendai, Japan; schroeder.marcin.e4@tohoku.ac.jp.

MARCIN STRZELECKI. Music theorist and composer, instrumentalist, Academy of Music in Kraków, Poland.

KONRAD SZACIŁOWSKI. Professor of chemistry, philatelist, AGH University of Science and Technology, Kraków, Poland.

BERND ULMANN. Professor for business informatics at the "Hochschule für Oekonomie und Management" in Frankfurt/Main, Germany; guest professor and lecturer at the Institute of Medical Systems Biology at Ulm University; ulmann@analogparadigm.com.

JORDI VALLVERDÚ. ICREA Acadèmia Researcher at Universitat Autònoma de Barcelona.

Conception and layout on InDesign Johanna Blayac & Louis-José Lestocart.